FORGIVE ME, PLEASE

Patricia Velasquez

Copyright © 2022 by Patricia Velasquez

All rights reserved.

No portion of this book may be reproduced in any form without written permission from the publisher or author, except as permitted by U.S. copyright law.

Contents

Prologue	1
1. Chapter 1	5
2. Chapter 2	10
3. Chapter 3	14
4. Chapter 4	19
5. Chapter 5	23
6. Chapter 6	27
7. Chapter 7	31
8. Chapter 8	35
9. Chapter 9	40
10. Chapter 10	44
11. Chapter 11	48
12. Chapter 12	52
13. Chapter 13	56
14. Chapter 14	60
15. Chapter 15	64

16.	Chapter 16	68
17.	Chapter 17	72
18.	Chapter 18	76
19.	Chapter 19	80
20.	Chapter 20	85
21.	Chapter 21	89
22.	Chapter 22	93
	Epilogue	97

Prologue

Cameron's POV

April 2005

I can't believe it, there is two lines on the test, two pink line that mean so much to me. I'm pregnant. I'm actually pregnant, that explains the sore breast, being tired and craving hot chips with tomato sauce. Not to mention the heighten sense of smell. I can't wait till my husband Keith comes home so I can share the news with him.

Keith is a business man, he took over his parents company just after marrying me. The business was Young industries and was a multibillion dollar company. When I met Keith I had no idea who he was. I was a young woman from a small town near Forster. We met when I finished uni after studying business and was trying to get a job. I literally ran into him trying to get out of the rain. I had come to the city giving myself two months to find a job and a place or to give up of my dream of making it big. I got a job the next week and Keith and I began a relationship together. It was a whirlwind romance and we had been happily married for just over two years now.

I was so excited to tell Keith and his family. I knew that his mother would be ecstatic, she had been hinting for over a year that she needed grand babies to spoil and that she wasn't getting younger. Keith and I had decided that once I had children I would be a stay at home mum and until then I worked on a side business which was kept out of the spotlight so I could create my business solely on my own merit.

My business was literally a part time job but I enjoyed it. I screen printed custom shirts and things all by hand. I didn't want it to be huge because I enjoyed helping my husband and being with him when he traveled so it was more a hobby. After we were married I had left my job as the hours were demanding and Keith had to travel a lot.

I was organising a special dinner with the announcement of the pregnancy to come with dessert. It was coming together nicely and Keith would be home in an hour. I was making his favourite, simple chicken wrapped in prosciutto stuffed with Brie cheese and a nice side salad with creamy mustard dressing. I had just put the chicken in the oven and was going to shower and change into something nice. I headed up to shower and quickly dressed and did my hair and make up before the buzzer indicating the chicken was ready went off.

I headed downstairs and grabbed out the chicken serving it for both Keith and I and then I waited. I knew that Keith would be home any minute now and I couldn't contain my excitement. The dessert was a simple chocolate cake with ice cream but I would give him a cute little baby romper which I screen printed myself saying "Due January 2006". The door opened and in walked Keith with one of my best friends Sarah. Keith didn't seem happy at all and I wasn't sure what was going on.

Keith stood in front of me "you are fucken disgusting. I can't believe I ever married you. You are nothing but a gold digging whore" he spat. "What?" I asked. I had no idea what he was talking about. "You heard me. You are a fucken useless whore, you won't get a fucken cent from me" he screamed.

I backed away from him and looked at Sarah who was comforting Keith. What the fuck was going on? "Keith what are you talking about?" I asked. I was genuinely confused. "I'm talking about my slut of a fucken wife. Did you think I wouldn't find out? Did you think that I was fucken stupid?" He laughed like a maniac and I was getting scared. This wasn't the husband I knew at all. He was throwing things around the room including the food I had made while screaming horrible things. He threw a cup at me hitting me in the arm "Stop it Keith or I'm calling the police" I screamed. I had never been so scared in my life. He had never once been violent and now he was throwing things at me. He picked up chairs and begun throwing those and I had no choice but to call the police who were there within minutes.

As I was talking to the police his family arrived and were glaring at me calling me every name under the sun. I had no idea what was going on but I was a shaking mess. I knew the stress wasn't good for the baby. I explained to the police I was scared and pregnant and had no where to go in the city as I wasn't from here and my family were four hours away.

The police advised that Keith had to leave for the night as he was the aggressor which made things worse. Keith came storming towards me hitting me across the face which caused me to fall. I grabbed my stomach hoping he hadn't hurt my baby before he was arrested on the spot and escorted out of the house calling out "that bastard isn't my child, I won't be paying a cent to support that thing". His mother and father were straight after him but not before his mother calling me a filthy whore. Sarah just smiled at me before following after my in-laws.

An ambulance was sent to check me out and I was asked if I wanted to press chargers which I had agreed to. I would never let a man abuse me like that nor would I risk my child to a man who could abuse his own wife. After deeming me ok the ambulance left along with the police. That's when I broke down sobbing. I had no idea what the hell had gone on and how my once loving husband turned like that.

I called my parents and told them what had happened and that I was pregnant with his child. They begged me to come home to them. I was exhausted emotionally and physically and didn't want to make a decision without thinking things through. I promised to call them in the morning and took myself to bed.

Chapter 1

Cameron's POV

I didn't get much sleep that night. I had spent most of it crying and trying to work out what was going on. I managed to get a little sleep dozing off at 4am only to be woken at 6am by my phone ringing. "Hello" I croaked I into the phone. "Cam, turn the news on now. What the hell is going on?" My brother Phillip asked me.

I grabbed the remote turning on the tv and there was my wedding photo with a split down the middle. The reports were that Keith and I split because I was apparently having an affair with some guy I didn't know. Next minute my in laws were on the tv claiming I made up the abuse and that's why Keith had been arrested. Sarah was on tv with them telling the whole world about my supposed affair and how she had begged me not to do it because my husband loved me so much. "What the actual fuck?" I said. "Cameron what the hell happened?" My brother asked. "Phil I don't know. I don't know. I'm pregnant Phil with his baby and he hit me last night. I don't even know the guy they claim I slept with. Phil what am I going to do?" I cried to my brother.

I had been on the phone to my brother for 15 minutes before there was a knock at the door. I quickly shoved my robe on and headed downstairs to see who was the door. I looked through the peephole and saw my brother in law Keiran. I opened the door allowing him in. Before closing and locking the door. There was paparazzi lining the street near my home.

"What are you doing here Keiran?" I asked. "Shit Cam, did he do all this?" Keiran asked. I just nodded my head. "Did he hurt you?" He asked before stepping closer and grabbing my chin "he hit you?" He asked. I pulled my face out of his hand "what's it matter? Why the hell are you here?" I asked again. "I don't believe what they are saying. Fuck Cameron, I know you and I know for a fact that you aren't after my brothers money. I also know you are madly in love with him and would never cheat. What the fuck is going on?" He asked me. "I don't know Keiran. I really don't know" I said before I had to run to the bathroom.

I just made it to the bathroom spewing up bile into the toilet. Great morning sickness, just what I need today. I flush the toilet and swing around to see Keiran looking at me. I excuse myself upstairs to my bathroom and brush my teeth gagging while doing so before I head back down seeing Keiran starting to clean up the mess. He picked up the box which contained the romper opening the lid. He pulled out the romper "your pregnant?" I nodded my head. "Does he know?" Keiran asked. "Yeh he told me it wasn't his and he wouldn't be giving me a cent" I said before bursting into tears.

What the hell was I going to do? I had no real money to set myself up here. I had no support in the city, my family was hours away and I couldn't move my stuff back to my parents place without money. I sure as hell wasn't taking my husbands money.

Keiran tried to comfort me but it only made me cry more. My phone was blowing up with text messages from my so called friends calling me every name under the sun not to mention my husband telling me I had 12 hours to get my shit out of his house before he would destroy it all and me. I knew I had to leave everything behind and use the few hundred dollars I had in my account to pay the people back who had ordered from me. I had just did a big order of supplies leaving me with less than $800 in my account and that would go to paying people back for the orders I wouldn't be able to fulfil.

After a good half hour crying, I picked myself up and told Keiran my plan. I would shower pack a bag, pay back the money to the orders I couldn't fulfil and make my way to my parents house. Keiran tried to get me to stay saying Keith would wake up and realise his mistake but I couldn't trust him after he became violent. Keiran asked me to move in with him until Keith woke up to him self, but I knew Keith and there was no coming back from this. Not for me anyway. I needed to be away from him at all costs.

I headed upstairs to shower and pack while Keiran said he would make some calls then drop me to the bus station so I could get the bus to my home town where my parents would be waiting. I was grateful for that at least. I packed my bag first just taking stuff I had paid for myself, I put my wedding ring and engagement ring on the night stand before heading to the shower.

Once I was done I headed downstairs seeing Keiran on the phone organising something. He pointed to the sandwich on the table and walked into the other room still talking on the phone. I hadn't eaten and didn't feel like eating but knew I needed to. I sat down slowing eating my sandwich until Keiran returned. "I organised a truck to be here in an hour. Your screen printing stuff will be loaded today and delivered to your parents place tomorrow. I also organised a car for you" Keiran started but I stopped him. "No Keiran, I can't afford any of this and I'm not using his money. Just let it go please" I said.

"Cameron this isn't his money, this is from me. Think of it as a present to my future niece or nephew ok. I'm sorry the child's father and his family is fucked up. Please let me be in the baby's life" Keiran asked. I was shocked, did he actually believe me. "I know that baby you are carrying is my brothers Cameron. He may want to throw that away but I'm not willing to" Keiran stated. I just nodded my head yes before bursting into tears again, pregnancy hormones suck.

Another hour went past and the car was delivered. Keiran even got a friend to act as a decoy so I could get away without the media knowing it was me and where I was going. He destroyed my current phone and had his friend get me a new one setting it up for me with a new number.

It was now time for me to leave. My equipment had been packed up I a truck and the guys promised it would be delivered tomorrow. I rang my mum letting her know I was going to be driving up today and would be there soon. I said my goodbyes to Keiran with him promising to keep in touch before I headed to the car and taking off towards my mums place leaving my old life behind.

Chapter 2

Cameron's POV

After five hours because of toilet breaks I made it to my parents house in Elizabeth beach. My dad met me at the car pulling me into a hug followed by my mum. My brother was at work at the local garage. He owned it and was the head mechanic. He didn't live with mum and dad anymore but his house literally was at the back of mum and dads place. I was sobbing into my mothers chest as she lead me upstairs and into the lounge room sitting me on the couch. My dad soon joined saying he would unpack the car shortly but wanting to hear what had happened.

I had covered the bruise on my face with some concealer because I knew shit was going to hit the fan when my dad and brother found out that Keith had laid a hand on me. My mum made some tea for us all and we sat with me focusing on my tea and mum making small talk about the drive up. I honestly couldn't really tell you how I drove here, it was mainly a blur which was scary. I shouldn't of been driving in my state but I had to put as much distance as I could between me and Keith because I didn't doubt for one second he would follow through with the threats he had made while telling me to get out of his house.

An hour after the small talk my brother came in looking at me with worry in his eyes. He pulled me into a hug "I knew that dickhead wasn't good enough for you" Phillip said to me making me smile. I knew now was the time to come clean with everything so I did.

I told them all about what had gone down the night before including Keith hitting me. To say my father and my brother were fuming was an understatement, mum had to stop both of them getting in the car to go see Keith and rearrange his face. I also said my business stuff would be here tomorrow and I would need to find somewhere to set up because I had to work my arse off to support my baby when it arrived. There was no doubt in my mind that I was going to keep this baby. My brother offered me room at the back of his mechanics. There was office space back there they never used so he said I could use it till I found somewhere else. I was so grateful for my family because I was going to be relying on them a lot now that me and my baby were on our own.

It was close to midnight when I headed to bed in my old room. I was physically and emotionally exhausted but I knew I had to be strong because this just wasn't about me anymore. Before falling asleep I text Keiran giving him the address to send my screen printing equipment to which he responded saying he would let them know and he hoped we were safe. With that I drifted to a restless sleep.

The next morning I got up early and morning sickness hit me again. I headed to work with my brother. I needed to check out the space which I was going to be running the business from. It needed to be cleaned but it would work. I had 4 hours to get it ready for the equipment to be dropped off so I pulled up my big girl panties and put my rubber gloves on before getting to work scrubbing the walls and floors. I liked to work in clean spaces. I sketched quickly were everything was going to go because Keiran had let me know the guys would be setting up the equipment for me before sitting down to eat a quick bite to eat. All I wanted was hot chips and tomato sauce so I walked over to the fish shop grabbing exactly that and a chocolate milk. I headed back to my brothers work sitting under one of the trees with my food to wait for the truck.

My brother sat next to me chuckling "pregnancy cravings already?" He asked. I just nodded, this wasn't the food I usually ate, in fact I never really cared for tomato sauce at all but now I could literally use a full bottle on my chips and still need more. It was so bloody good. Phil just shook his head "remind me to stock up on tomato sauce and chocolate milk when we head into town" he said. I just nodded still munching on my chips.

"How are you Cam? Like really how are you holding up?" He said. I went to answer but stopped myself. How was I? I knew I had to be strong for me and the baby but how was I really feeling about it all? "I feel so lost Phil. I don't know what went wrong or why he turned like that. I still don't know what happened but he just kept saying I was a gold digging whore. The worst part Sarah was all smug about it supporting him while he was hurting me. I lost my marriage. I'm alone with a baby that he claims isn't his and I don't know what to do.

I know I need to be strong for me and the baby but I feel broken and betrayed. He hit me Phil, the man I loved literally hit me wanting to cause me damage. Don't even get me started on the media and what they are saying" I said to my brother. Phil pulled me into a hug and I began to sob in my big brothers arms. How had everything gone so horribly wrong? Where was I going to go now? Could I really raise a baby on my own?

Ten minutes later and the truck was pulling in. I got up dusted myself off and got to work. I had my 20 minute break down now I needed to get up and get on with it. I had no one to rely on now so I had to rely on myself. The guys set it up within 2 hours connecting all the stuff together and securing the shelves to the wall. They also set up my computer before heading off to make the drive back to Sydney. I began to organise all the stocks and inks on the selves labelling things as I went and soon my brother was knocking telling me it was time to head home. He was impressed with my set up and I was proud I had achieved this much when all I wanted to do was crawl into a ball and forget about the real world for a while.

Chapter 3

Cameron's POV

July 2005

I can't believe today is my first scan, to say I'm excited is an understatement. My dad took the day off work and was going to come with me and my mum to the scan.

Time had flown by and my business was doing well. I had hired a lawyer to deal with Keith and the legal stuff so I wouldn't have to and within the week of hiring my lawyer I had my first lot of papers from Keith stating that he would not be financially responsible for any child I was to give birth to. I instructed my lawyer that I wanted amendments made that he would not seek custody of any children I was to birth at all and I would agree to taking no financial support for myself or my child. Within the hour of asking it came back with him agreeing. I was hurt by that but I didn't dwell on it at all. I had to just get on with my life.

My business was doing well and I ended up employing two teenagers to help out after school a few afternoons and Saturdays. I opened up my orders and my business had taken off. I was getting in more stock weekly to keep up with demand and on Sundays mum and I had stalls at the different farmers markets in different towns. I was selling my prints and tie dyed babies clothes which were a hit. Monday and Tuesday were now my weekends. I had so many orders to pack and ship that the girls I employed would literally pack the orders 2 afternoons a week for me and on Saturdays Tammy would help with the printing while Sage would pack the clothes into crates and into my brothers ute so we could transport them to the market on Sunday morning sometimes leaving at 4am to get there and set up by 7 when the markets started. It's was hard work but I knew I would need to slow down once the baby arrived so I had to make money and get established now.

I kept in contact with Keiran through text and he was happy that my business was taking off. I had offered to pay him back for the moving cost of my equipment but he wouldn't have it at all. Him and I never talked about Keith and I was thankful for that. It was hard enough seeing him on different magazines with his new girl each week.

The police had settled out of court for the assault against me with Keith agreeing to seek help for anger issues and to stay away from me. His mother and father sprouted to the media that I had made it all up and therefore the police had dropped the case. They also publicly disowned the baby I was carrying saying it was a bastard child and I had tricked there son into marry me stating I was pregnant when I wasn't which was a lie. They also went on to say they didn't believe I was actually pregnant at all and that I had made it all up just to try to keep Keith to use him for his money. I ultimately didn't care anymore. I didn't want toxic people in my life nor the life of my baby.

No one knew where I was expect for Keiran and he had sworn to keep my location secret from his family and the media. I had returned to using my maiden name and being a little town off the beaten track most people wouldn't think to look for me here. It helped that no one knew I grew up here at all. We had kept that private to protect my family for the media's attention.

We were on our way to John Hunter hospital which is where I would give birth to my baby. I was going to have my 12 week scan today and meet the midwife team who would be in charge of my pregnancy. They were a group of 5 midwives who would oversee the pregnancy and one of them would deliver my baby. I had wanted a natural water birth if I could. I had been reading about calm birthing and I wanted to try it at least. I was the one in charge now and I could do what I wanted without having to get approval from anyone. I also didn't have to worry about the media following me while I was in labour anymore. It was an hour and a half drive from my parents place in Elizabeth beach but I'm sure there would be plenty of time to get to the hospital when the time came.

We parked the car and headed into the maternity area me looking around taking everything in. First I would meet the midwives then I would get my scan. I checked in with the midwives giving them medical history of myself and they took my weight and height, blood pressure the date of my last period and spoke to me about what sort of birth I wanted. They asked who would be my support person and I informed them that it would be my mum and dad and my brother was a backup person. They asked about the father and I informed them he wasn't on the scene. I didn't go into to much detail but I asked that my records remain private as there was a risk of the father finding me. They assured me that they followed strict privacy policies and my records would be sealed. I met Lucy and Beth two of the midwives in the group and learnt that Jane, Cassidy and Tara were the other three in the group. We scheduled my next on-site appointment for after the 20 week scan. The 16 week check up could be done at my local maternal clinic in Forster which was run by the midwives so I wouldn't have to travel before I was sent down for my first ultrasound.

When my name was called mum, dad and I headed into the room and I hoped on the table. The girl Claire was lovely and bubbly which made me more excited to see my baby for the first time. She lifted my shirt and put the cold gel on my stomach before she got to work. "So do twins run in the family?" She asked. There on the screen was two babies not one.

Mum squeezed my hand as a tear run down my face. My babies were on the screen and I couldn't be happier seeing them. "Umm sorry what?" I asked. I could see two babies on the screen but it was still a shock. Claire laughed and explained she would need to let my midwife team know. She took the measurements and confirmed I was due early February next year before she printed out some shots of my babies for me. "I'm having twins" I whispered to myself. "My little girls is having two babies" my dad said before we all laughed together.

We had to head back to the midwife team and discuss the risks and possibly send me to the doctor for some of my future appointments. Twins meant it could be a high risk pregnancy. I learnt I was having fraternal twins meaning I could have two girls, two boys or a boy and a girl. I didn't really care as long as they came out healthy. I would love them no matter what. Once finished we headed back home to tell my brother the good news.

Chapter 4

Cameron's POV

I am currently 24 weeks pregnant and I look like I swallowed a watermelon. We are heading to my appointment at John hunter Hospital. I feel like a whale but I wouldn't change a thing. I get tired easily and it's hard to tie my shoelaces but I make it work.

My pregnancy has been going well so far. I stopped vomiting about 16 weeks along and the twins are measuring well. They were on the smaller side during the 20 week ultrasound but the doctor assured me that was ok. Keiran had been so surprised that I was having twins, he sent two massive teddy bears to my parents house for the twins. He begged me to find out the gender but I didn't want to. I wanted it to be a surprise for all my hard work. Something to look forward to after the 9 months carrying them. We had gotten really close and spoke to each other every day. He asked all about my baby bump and how I was doing in general. He had sent several gift baskets to me with little treats and cute little gender neutral things for the babies. I even printed a onesie line for uncles which he adored and ended up buying some for my twins. The ones he chose were "uncles best friend" and "if you think I'm cute wait till you see my uncle". I laughed when I saw the order from him.

Business is booming and I have given up going to the markets weekly. I open my office space up once a week now on Saturdays for people to come past and buy directly from me. It was to difficult to continue to do the markets while I'm pregnant. I do still do the pacific palms markets though considering they are literally across the road from my brothers house. He sets it all up for me and mum and I man the store. I have regulars who come past just to see my bump and usually end up buying little outfits from me. I also extended my range to include kids clothes.

Sage still helps out after school and Saturdays and has offered to run my setup for me when the babies arrive. She finishes year 12 at the end of the year and wants to take a year off uni but her parents have said she needs a job. I have been training her how to print the designs and she already is hands on with the tie dye so I am going to offer her the position. I will be still around and working part time. My mum had offered to help with the twins and they will attend daycare when they are old enough.

I have also looked at moving to a bigger warehouse because the office is getting way to crowded with the supplies I need. My brother owns the land that I'm using so I literally have no overheads for the business besides me internet and electricity. He has offered to check the cost of extending the space I have now so I could stay where I am. It's close to home meaning I could be at work and the twins could be home with my mum and it's only a 3 minute drive away. It's also a great place for people to see me as they drive past and I could even have a shop front so I could be selling every day. I would have to take out a business loan to fund the extension and then once that was done I would have to employ permanent staff as I would need a few working the printing stations and running the shop but that is a dream at the moment.

Keiran was going to be meeting us for the appointment today and my mum was concerned that Keith would be there. I had no reason not to trust Keiran though and I doubt Keith would be bothering me at all. Last the magazine reported was he and Sarah were now a thing because I betrayed them both. Keiran wanted to see my baby bump and had offered to come with me to look at prams and car seats for the twins. There wasn't a lot in Forster so being in Newcastle meant more places to look and I could actually physically see them and feel them rather than just ordering online.

I hadn't budgeted for twins but I knew I would make it work no matter what and I had been working a lot more to come up with the money for everything I needed for the twins. I would have to double everything and that was going to be pricey but I didn't mind at all. I myself didn't need much and was literally living in dresses that I was making myself and printing and dying along with some cheap Kmart tights as it was winter. I rarely wore shoes these days because my feet were usually swollen.

When we pulled up to the hospital I spotted Keiran right away calling out to him as I got out of the car. "Oh my god, look at you. Look at this bump. That's my nieces in there. It's uncle Keiran babies" he said. Keiran was convinced I was having twin girls and that they would be the mini versions of me. He told me it was his gut feeling. "They could also be your nephews in there or a niece and a nephew Keiran" I replied. "Nonsense. I know what I'm talking about" he replied.

We headed into my appointment with me making introductions. Today Lucy was here for my appointment. She measured my stomach, took my blood pressure and then asked if Keiran wanted to hear the babies heart beat. He eagerly agreed and I got up on the bed lifting my dress over my stomach for Lucy to use the Doppler. We found twin one right away and Keiran was amazed before we moved onto twin two who usually liked to hide. Much to both our amazement twin 2 wasn't hiding today and we got the heartbeat pretty quickly. I booked my glucose test for 28 weeks and said goodbye before we headed to the baby store to look for prams and car seats.

Chapter 5

Cameron's POV

I'm currently 30 weeks pregnant and just got off the phone to Keiran. He had purchased the twin donkey bugaboo pram for me and I was so grateful yet so annoyed at him for spending that money. He told me it was a gift to his nieces. He also brought me the car capsules that attach to the pram. I was a sobbing mess on the phone to him. He assured me that it was nothing.

We spoke for a while before he warned me that Keith had hired a private investigator to search for something. He wasn't sure what but that was the first time he had said anything to me about Keith. He had never once mentioned him before the entire time since I left the city and Keith. I thought nothing of it to be honest. He had moved on and I was to busy to dwell on what happened. I needed to focus on myself and the twins. Keith was in the past and once we reached the 1 year and 1 day mark we could be legally divorced.

I got off the phone to Keiran and finished up the order I was working on. By the time I was finished it was close to 7.30pm and I was beyond exhausted. I was still living with my parents and they had been the best of help to me. I didn't know how I was going to repay them at all.

We had decided the granny flat downstairs at my parents place, would be turned into my room and the nursery because it would be easier being downstairs with newborn babies by myself getting them to and from the car and it also had more room to fit everything in. I would still be upstairs with the babies when someone could help me up there and we would be having our meals upstairs but this way not everyone would have to be up during the night when the twins were up. Dad still had work and I didn't think it was fair for him to be disturbed all the time with me having to feed in the middle of the night.

We had painted the downstairs and set it up with a microwave, fridge, rocking chair, a queen bed for me, change table, two cots and two chest of draws. There was also room for a couch and TV which I had yet to order. My brother and dad had started to put everything together for me just incase. I had also been buying nappies and wipes with each grocery shop so I had a stash when the babies arrived.

I locked up my work space with Sage and then we both headed out, Sage lived near blueys beach and like most kids out here had her own car. I headed off home and dragged myself upstairs. I was going to eat dinner and then shower before falling into bed. When I got upstairs my parents were watching the news. "Cam, have you heard the news tonight?" Dad asked me. "Nope I'm exhausted, had a massive order to finish. I'm going to eat, shower then head to bed" I replied. Just then my brother came running up the back stairs to my parents house bursting into the room. "Cameron you need to see the news" he said before going onto my parents computer and getting onto whatever he wanted me to see.

I walked over and there on the screen was Keith. "Why do I need to see this?" I asked. "Just watch" Phil replied. "Keith is it true you found out that Sarah orchestrated the entire scandal causing you to seperate from your wife after you allegedly assaulted her?" Asked a reporter. "Sarah did in fact orchestrate the entire thing" he replied. "Keith is it true your wife is pregnant with your child and you have no idea where she is or how the baby is?" Another reported asked. "I am unsure if she is pregnant or not. She did inform me she was pregnant before we seperated but I am unsure how or if the pregnancy progressed" he stated.

"Keith our sources say she is in fact very much pregnant with your child however you have signed your rights away to any child she is to birth. What do you have to say about that? Also where is your wife now? Are you still in the process of getting a divorce?" A report asked. "We are not getting divorced. I love my wife very much. This has all been a misunderstanding that's all" he replied.

I slammed the computer shut. "A misunderstanding? Ha. He has got to be kidding. The divorce will be going ahead. I can't deal with this now I'm going to shower and go to bed" I say before heading up to the bathroom. I'm no longer hungry.

I take my time in the shower. My back is killing me and the water seems to be helping. I sing to my babies while showering which makes them settle down and stop moving so much. They are always so active and it can be painful, there isn't much more room in there so I often get a kick in the ribs which hurts.

Twin 2 is also laying on my spine which can be painful. Tonight I know I'll be using the wheat bag to place on my lower back. I usually reheat the bag during the night on one of my many toilet trips. Twins on your bladder isn't the most fun especially when it wakes you at least three times a night. Once out of the shower I head to my room grabbing my wheat pack and heading to the kitchen to warm it up. I hear my phone ringing in my room but I couldn't be bothered going to answer it. I say goodnight to my family again who are deep in conversation before heading up to bed.

I check my phone and see it's Keiran who called me but I'm way to exhausted to have a conversation with him now. I get into bed cuddling my body mate pillow and tuck my wheat pack into the back of my pants so it's is resting on my lower back before trying to get some much needed sleep. I have tomorrow off so I don't need to set and alarm. I plan on sleeping most of tomorrow because carrying two babies is exhausting as hell. I soon doze off and I welcome the sleep.

Chapter 6

Cameron's POV

I wake up about 10am the next morning. I was up a few times during the night to pee but at 10am I was hungry so decided it was time to get up. I roll myself out of bed and head straight to the bathroom. I do my business and then check my phone seeing multiple calls from Keiran. It must be important so while I'm heading downstairs I call him back. He answers on the first ring.

"Cameron, where are you? Are you ok?" He rushes out. "Calm down, I'm fine. I was just sleeping. I worked 10 hours yesterday and I was exhausted and in pain. I'm at my parents place and having a much needed day off" I reply. I get down the stairs and look out the glass doors only to see Keith standing there looking at me. "Cameron, Keith knows where you are he is on his way. You need to head somewhere else before he gets there" he says. "Ahh to late" I reply. "What do you mean to late? Cameron, I'm literally turning onto the lakes way now. I'll be there as soon as I can. Just go somewhere till I get there" he rushes out. "He is here" I reply.

Keith is standing on the other side of the glass door looking at me well more like staring at me and I'm staring right back. What the hell is he doing here? "Cameron open the door" Keith calls out. "Shit Cameron can you hide somewhere?" Keiran asks. "Bit late. He is looking right at me" I reply. Where the hell is my mum and dad when you need them?

"Cameron please just open the door I want to talk to you" Keith calls out. "Shit is that him" Keiran asks. "Yep" I reply. "Cameron please open the door. I just want to talk to you. Baby please" he begs out. I shake my head no. I don't trust him at all after the last time I saw him. "Keiran I think I'm here alone. I need to go so I can call my brother and see if he can come over" I say before hanging up. I know the lakes way and Keiran won't be here for at least 40 minutes.

I walk over to the kitchen with Keith watching my every move. I dial my brothers number and he picks up after several rings "hey Cam, how you feeling today?" He asks. "Phil are you home?" I ask quickly. Keith is still at the door begging me to let him in. That is the only way out unless I go upstairs and on to the verandah then climb down from there. I don't think that's a smart choice seeing I'm heavily pregnant with twins.

"No I'm in town. What's up?" Phil asks. "Shit" I reply. "Cameron what's going on?" Phil asks me. "Keith turned up on the door step and now he is begging me to let him in. Mum and dad don't seem to be here. I'm scared Phil. What if he is here to hurt me? Keiran just turned onto the lakes way but he won't be here for at least half an hour. What do I do?" I ask my brother. "Hey first off you need to calm down. The stress isn't good for the babies. Second tell him he needs to leave or you will call the police. I'm heading back now and will call a few of my mates in the area to see if anyone is close that can come over and be there before me. Whatever you do Cameron don't let him in. Do you hear me? Don't let him in and keep the door locked" Phil says. "Ok" I whisper still not taking my eyes off Keith.

Phil hangs up and now I need to wait for someone to turn up. "Cameron baby please open the door. I just want to talk to you please" Keith calls out again. I head closer to the door making sure the door is actually locked. "That's it baby, open the door so we can work this out" Keith calls out. I scoff, there is nothing to work out at all. We are done and dusted, you and I signed documents attesting to the fact that you had no legal claim over any child I birthed and I had no legal claim for financial support.

"Go away Keith. I have nothing to say to you. You aren't welcome here and I will call the police if you don't leave" I say firmly. "Cameron please. I'm sorry. It was a misunderstanding" he says. "There was no misunderstanding Keith. You hit me. You threw things at me and then threatened that if I didn't leave you would harm my unborn child and destroy me. There is no misunderstanding that" I replied. Did this dude have rocks in his head or what?

Keith was quiet for a few minutes before looking at me "Sarah convinced me you cheated on me. She showed me text messages and pictures. She convinced me you were using me for my money. I believed her. I'm so sorry Cameron. I should of known it wasn't true but she told me and said you wanted her help to take me and my family down" he said. I shook my head at Keith. I trusted Sarah how could she? More importantly my own husband believed her over his wife.

"That isn't an excuse Keith. You put your hands on me in temper. You assaulted me and I won't ever forgive that. Please leave" I said. I wasn't going to cry in front of him. I wouldn't give him the satisfaction. "You are carrying my baby Cameron. I won't ever leave. I have a right to know my child love" he said. "You signed that right away Keith and I'm not your love anymore. You need to leave now before I call the police, you still have an undertaking to the court saying you will stay away from me" I replied. "Fuck the undertaking Cameron you are my wife and that's my child. Don't do this please baby. I made a mistake a huge one but please don't punish me like this" he said.

Chapter 7

Cameron's POV

I closed the blinds so I could no longer see Keith and he could no longer see me. I could still hear him though so I turned on some music. I made myself some toast knowing I had to eat because I hadn't eaten the night before and then began to eat. I started to get some tightening of my stomach. I just assumed it was the babies moving but it was getting a little painful.

I finished my breakfast and headed up stairs to get changed but had to stop because I was getting more cramp like pains in my stomach. I called the midwives "Jane speaking" Jane answered the phone. "Jane it's Cameron, I'm getting some tightening in my stomach" I said into the phone. "Ok, is it making you stop what you are doing? And how far along are you now?" Jane asked. "I'm 30 weeks and to start with it wasn't but they are getting stronger and I just had to stop walking up the stairs" I replied. "Ok and how far apart are they roughly" Jane asked. "About every 8 to 10 minutes" I replied. "Ok mumma I want you to head in. It may be nothing but you are carrying twins so I would prefer to check you out" Jane stated. "Ok.

It will take me a while though" I replied. "No problems. If they get worse call an ambulance. See you when you get here Cameron" Jane replied. "Thanks Jane see you soon" I said.

Well shit. I was here by myself and had to get to John Hunter. I had started packing a hospital bag but thought I had more time. I finished putting things in the bag for myself and the twins. I grabbed my body mate pillow and headed downstairs. I decided to head to the bathroom and put a pad on just in case and grabbed a few towels for the car incase my water broke on the way. I even grabbed a few snacks and a bucket incase I vomited. My hands were full so I placed everything besides my pillow and towels on the floor near the door.

I opened the blinds to see my brother and Keiran talking well more like yelling at Keith. I unlocked the door and all eyes snapped to me just as I got another cramp in my stomach. I dropped the towels and was hugging the pillow and groaning. I wasn't going to admit these were contractions yet, it was way to early and I wasn't ready.

"Shit Cameron" Phil said coming towards me. I grabbed onto his arm for support and within a minute the pain had stopped "hospital now" I said. Phil nodded "shit Cam, isn't it to early?" Keiran asked. I just nodded my head before picking up my bag. I also had to get everything else. I didn't even look at Keith.

"Here Cam give me the bag and your hand. We will call mum and dad on the way" Phil said. "I'll take her. She is my wife" Keith said. I rolled my eyes and handed Phil the bag. "Let me get the other stuff" Keiran said. He picked everything up and went to take my pillow but I wanted to hold it, it was protecting my babies from Keith. I stepped out of the door, before waddling to the stairs. "Phil lock the door" I said as I slowly made my way down the stairs.

I headed towards Phil's car which was at the top of the drive way walking slowly. "Here Cam, let me help you into my car" Keith said trying to take my arm. I pulled it away "don't touch me" I replied. "Please baby we need to go to the hospital get our baby checked" Keith replied. I shook my head and continued up the steep driveway towards the Ute. "Cam be careful" Phil called out and next minute Keiran was beside me.

I held his hand and slowly walked up the drive way "I'm scared" I whispered to him. "They will be fine. You will be fine. I promise" Keiran said. "Get your hands off my wife Keiran. She is coming in my car" Keith said. It was clear to see he was fuming. "Don't listen to him Cam, focus on your babies" Keiran stated.

"Cam I got to stop for petrol on the way" Phil said just as another contraction hit making me groan out in pain. "I don't think that's going to work Phil" Keiran said while I clamped down on his arm. "We will take my car" Keiran gritted out while I squeezed his hand. "Put my wife in my car. I'm driving her and my baby" Keith said. "Shut up Keith. Shut up and go home. These are my babies you'd do well to remember that" I yelled out.

That one hurt and I'm now classing them as contractions. Keiran looked at me like he was proud and my brother jogged up to me. "Babies? As in more than one?" Keith asked. "Go home Keith" I replied. "We are having more than one baby? Cam you have made me the happiest man alive" Keith said. "We are not having anything

Keith. Talk to your lawyer. Hurry up and open this door Keiran I need to get to the hospital now" I told them.

Keiran opened the boot chucking everything in "I need the bucket and towels in case" I said so he grabbed those out while I got in the front seat and Phil hopped in the back. Phil was on the phone to my mum and dad who were out in the lake fishing. They would meet us at the hospital. Keiran got into the drivers seat and Keith was standing on the drive way shocked.

"Let's go" I said. Keiran started the car which seemed to jump start Keith as he came running towards the car. "I'm not sitting in a car with him for over an hour in labour so move" I said. Keiran locked the doors and started to head off. I saw Keith in my side mirror screaming something before he ran to his car jumping in. It was going to be a long drive. We hit the lakes way quickly and Keith was following us. My contractions were every 10-12 minutes only lasting about a minute. I knew it was to early for the babies to be born and I just wanted this all to go away. I didn't understand why Keith had turned up now.

Chapter 8

Cameron's POV

As we pull up to the hospital Phil helps me out of the car. I let them know to leave the stuff in the car and just grab my purse and my pillow. It has my pregnancy card in it. We headed towards the maternity area for me to check in with Keith trying to grab a hold of my hand. I don't even acknowledge anyone. I need to focus on keeping calm for myself and my babies.

I check in and am sent to the maternity suite where Jane is waiting for me. "Cameron who do we have here today with us?" She asks. I just shake my head no "ok mumma, let's get you into a room" she replies after seeing my face. "You three wait out here while she gets settled and I'll come get you in a minute" Jane says to them all. "I'm her husband and the babies father" Keith speaks up. Jane and the others know that I didn't want him finding out anything about the pregnancy because I was worried he would take my children. "And I'm the midwife in charge. You will wait out here like I have asked or I will have security escort you off the hospital property. Are we clear?" Jane asks. Keith nods his head and I'm placed in the room with Jane.

"Ok hop on the bed and I'll hook you up to the monitor to check the babies and we will then check to see if your in labour" Jane says. I get situated and she hooks up the monitors labelling twin one and twin two. Both heart beats are strong and I'm thankful for that. Jane checks if I am dilated which I'm not and my blood pressure which is slightly elevated, wonder why?

"The doctor will come and check you out but I don't think you are in labour. I think this was braxton hicks contractions. He might want to keep you in though for a while just to monitor you. I'll grab you some water. Anyone you want to allow in?" Jane asks. "Can you let my brother Phil in please?" I ask. "Sure try to relax it will help to lower your blood pressure" Jane says before leaving the room.

A few minutes later, Phil comes in. "How are you feeling? When do I get to meet my nieces or nephews? I'm not staying when you give birth though" he asks. I laugh at that, I wouldn't want my brother in the room while I'm birthing my babies. "They think it was a false alarm. My blood pressure is up no surprise there. The doctor is going to come check me out but I might be here for a while sorry" I reply. "Don't be mum and dad are on there way here so I can send Keith and Keiran home if you like" Phil states. I nod my head "Keiran has my stuff in his car and he can come in and say goodbye. But please keep Keith away" I reply. "Sure thing Cam. I'll be right back. Want anything?" I shake my head no.

About 10 minutes later there is a commotion outside my room and I'm still waiting for the doctor. "Cameron please baby we need to talk. Is that our babies heartbeat? Please baby let me in" Keith calls out.

Jane walks in with the doctor. "Hello Ms Tan. I am doctor Rosehorn, I am one of the Obstetricians on duty today. I'm just going to check you and your babies if that's ok?" The doctor asks. "Sure" I reply.

"Now the man out there is claiming to be your husband and wants to come in are you ok with him being here?" He asks. "He is my husband but we have separated and he doesn't want anything to do with the babies" I reply. "Right well that seems to have changed he is out there threatening my staff with a lawsuit if he isn't allowed to be in here and given your records" he replies. "I'm sorry. He has no claim to the babies" I reply getting upset.

"Hey Cameron calm down. I'll get your brother" Jane says. "So the babies are not biologically your husbands?" The doctor asks. "They are, he signed away his rights" I reply. "Hmm I doubt that" the doctor states. "Get out. Get out now" I scream. How dare he? How dare this stupid doctor say anything? He doesn't know what has gone on. "Ms Tan this is my maternity ward" the doctor states. "Fine" I reply.

I start taking the monitors off, I'm not staying here. Jane comes back in the room with Phil "what's going on?" She asks. "I won't be insulted by this man again. He isn't allowed to touch me. You have no idea what my husband did to me nor do you have any idea what has happened with my babies. How dare you?" I scream out. The door mustn't of been closed properly because next minute Keith and Keiran are in the delivery suite with me still taking all the monitors off. I have tears running down my face but I just want to get out of here.

"What the hell is going on?" Keiran asks. Keith is watching me rip everything off my body. I'm literally in my underwear and a sports bra. Don't judge clothing is uncomfortable when pregnant. "This stupid man thinks he knows everything. I won't let him touch me or my babies again. I won't be insulted by a small minded small dick man. I'm leaving, I'll birth these babies at home if I have to" I reply. That might sound unreasonable but I don't care at this point.

"What did you do to my wife?" Keith yells. "Mr Tan" the doctor starts to say. "It's Mr Young and this is my wife who you have upset" Keith yells. "Right well Mr Young, your wife here says you have no claim on the babies she indicated they weren't yours saying you signed them away. I merely pointed out this is my maturity unit" the stupid doctor says. "Get out doctor" Jane says. "He did get his lawyer to draw up papers, my sister had to sign saying he wasn't legally responsible for any baby my sister birthed as well as not being financially responsible. He was busy fucking other woman while my sister was pregnant after he assaulted her" Phil yelled out. I burst into tears again, my dirty laundry was all being hung out for all to see and hear. Keiran came over to me pulling me into a hug just as another pain ripped through my stomach causing me to yell out in pain.

"Doctor Rosehorn, you need to leave now. I will be reporting you to the head of the hospital. Cameron you need to get into bed. I believe these contractions are being brought on by stress and this is not good for those babies. Philip go to the desk and get me another midwife in here please it's urgent. As for you Mr Young, I think it's best you leave the room" Jane speaks with authority. "You heard her

Keiran you need to leave. Cameron doesn't need the stress" Keith says. "I was talking to you" Jane replies.

Chapter 9

Cameron's POV

All hell breaks loose and the duress alarm is pushed. The doctor and Keith are arguing with Jane. Midwives and doctors come flying into my room from everywhere and see the scene in front of them. A sobbing pregnant woman, a doctor and some guys arguing with the midwife and Phil trying to push Keith out of the room. Security is called and next minute the doctor and Keith are being dragged out of the room. Security is trying to get Phil out too but I'm begging them to let him stay, he didn't do anything wrong.

Phil comes back with one of the midwives and Jane takes her to the side speaking with her. The midwife I don't know, let's Jane know the head of the hospital and then head of the maturity department are coming before leaving and Jane heading back over to me. "Cameron I need you on the bed" she says.

I get on the bed and she starts connecting the monitors again. She takes my blood pressure which is higher now no surprise and hooks up the heart monitors for the babies. They are both steady which I'm grateful for. Phil is on the phone to mum and dad who have just arrived at the hospital. But they can't get into our room as I'm on lock down because of Keith causing a scene and the doctor. I have two security guards standing guard and no one is allowed in until the head of the hospital has been. So much for my calm birth.

I fell asleep soon after only to be woken by a new doctor coming into the room. "Hi Mrs Young, I am Doctor Laine but you can call me Shaun" the doctor says. "It's Ms Tan now but please call me Cameron" I reply. "Right, I'm the head of the maternity department here at John Hunter. I heard there was quiet a commotion here today" he states. "I am so sorry about that" I reply. "Don't be silly. I apologise on behalf of my doctor, he will be held accountable for his actions today and disciplinary action will be taken. You have quiet the entourage out there trying to get in" Shaun said. "Oh. You mean my mum and dad?" I asked. "And your mother and father in law, your husband and his lawyer. They are demanding access to your medical records and that you be moved to Sydney immediately" Shaun stated. "He has no legal calm to me or the babies, we are legally separated. He signed paper work waving his parental rights to any children I birth" I replied.

"Right do you have a copy of that? It might be a good idea to have it on file. Also it would be a good idea to have a legal next of kin for yourself and your children" Shaun says. "My lawyer does I'll call her and organise it to be sent over. Can you let my parents in please?" I ask. "Sure but let's get these babies checked first if you don't mind" Shaun said.

Phil and Keiran left the room so the doctor could check me out. After he was done he said "now Cameron, your blood pressure is a little high and I'm putting you on some blood pressure medication. I am also going to admit you overnight just to monitor your blood pressure and put you on some fluids. Jane can you get that started for me? I'll let your parents in and then we will get you a room and set you up for the night. I will come check on you in the morning and send you home if everything is ok. Your twins are doing well both have strong stable heartbeats and the contractions seemed to have settled when you are calm" Shaun said. I just nodded my head. "If you can, get your lawyer to send over that paper work and sort out a legal next of kin so the hospital has it on file. Try to get some rest Cameron" said before leaving the room.

Jane set up an IV hooking up some fluids for me and about 10 minutes later my mum and dad came into the room followed by Phil and Keiran. "She needs to keep calm, the contractions were stress induced. We are keeping her in overnight as her blood pressure is elevated just as a precaution but no more stress" Jane told them all.

Mum came over to me and gave me a hug while Dad thanked Jane. Keiran and Phil stood to the side watching me. "I'm ok guys. The babies heartbeats are strong and stable, look" I said pointing to the monitors. Both boys nodded.

"Mum I need you to call my lawyer and have her send over the paper work that Keith signed waving his rights to the babies. I also need my lawyer to draw up a legal next of kin document naming the four of you so Keith doesn't get a say if something happens to me" I said. "What?" Phil asked. "I know he has his lawyer here and is demanding my medical records and to have me moved. I get a say now because it's my body but legally I need someone named to make those decisions for me if I'm incapable and it will never be Keith. We are still legally married so it would fall to him. I trust all of you here to make those decisions for me and the babies if I can't" I replied. "I'll sort it now" dad said. "Thank you. Her number is in my phone. Oh Keiran are you ok with that? Also my bags, I will need them from your car please" I said. "No problem Cam. I won't let my brother near my nieces if something happens" he said. I just shook my head, he was so sure they would both be girls and yet we didn't actually know the gender of either babies.

Dad and Keiran left the room to do what I asked while mum, Phil and I discussed everything including the names I had picked for the babies if they were girls or boys. Soon dad and Keiran were back in the room and I was struggling to stay awake. Sleep soon took over me until it was time to move me to a ward.

Chapter 10

Cameron's POV

I was moved to a private room on the ward because apparently the media had got wind of me being here. Mum and dad were going to be heading home shortly and would be back in the morning to take me home. Phil was going with them when he got back from getting me food. I absolutely hated hospital food and all I wanted was hot chips with tomato sauce and an ice cold chocolate milk.

Phil returned with my chips and drink with Keiran following close behind holding a massive boutique of colourful flowers. He placed them down on the floor in the room and then handed me two teddies. "Flowers for you Cam and teddies for my nieces" he said before kissing my cheek.

Phil handed me my food and Keiran was horrified with the amount of tomato sauce I was using. Phil literally brought me a full bottle and everyone just laughed at Keiran's reaction. "Hey don't judge it's literal heaven" I said to Keiran. "Right pregnant women are weird" he replied.

We were interrupted by a knock at the door. "Come in" I called out. "Delivery for Mrs Young" the guy said. "Sorry wrong room" I said. "You are Cameron Young though? I was given this room number" the guy said. "I'm Cameron Tan" I replied. "The delivery is from your husband Keith Young" he replied. I shook my head and Keiran went over to get the delivery excusing the guy from the room. It was the biggest bunch of red roses I had ever seen, there had to be at least 4 dozen roses here with a love heart ballon and two teddies which were joined at the hand.

There was also a letter inside the bunch of flowers. I put the letter on the table, I would read it when no one else was around. Keiran placed the flowers around the room. Each dozen of roses had its own vase and the 4 vases joined together to make it look like one large bunch of flowers. I just rolled my eyes. That use to make my heart skip a beat and make me feel special, now it just made me feel cheap. Did he really think that roses would make me forgive him for everything he had done?

Just as everyone was leaving another delivery arrived of flowers and a fruit hamper. I was getting annoyed with Keith thinking he could buy his way back into my life. Keiran accepted the deliveries before looking at the card. These were from his parents and the card read "we miss you and can't wait to meet our beautiful grand babies love Maz and Max" my bloody in laws. Keiran set the flowers down on the floor next to the others and put the fruit basket on the table. "Take it with you. I don't want it" I told them. Dad picked it up before kissing me on the cheek and saying his goodbyes. "Tell them I'm not accepting anymore deliveries at the nurses station please" I called after them. I just wanted them to go back to leaving me and my babies alone. Flowers and gifts wasn't going to make me forget what they had done to me.

I turned the TV on and the news flashed on screen. There was a shot of the hospital I was at and I knew this story was going to be about me. There was Keith's lawyer and his parents talking to the media. "Can you confirm that Cameron is right at this moment giving birth?" The reporter asked. "We have no comment. Our daughter in law has asked for privacy. She is being taken care of by her team of doctors and the babies are doing well" my ex mother in law said. "So it is true Mrs Young is carrying twins? Can you confirm that Mr Young is currently with his wife?" The reporter asks. I switched the TV off and picked up my phone. I was going to get my lawyer to sort this out for good.

I had just gotten off the phone with my lawyer who was going to release a statement on my behalf. She was going to inform them that I had a scared during the pregnancy brought on by stress. She was going to deny all rumours of being back with Keith and ask the media for some privacy at this time to not cause more stress putting myself and my children at risk. She was also going to let them know that the babies were not ready to be born and that I still had a few months of the pregnancy left and that I wished Keith and his family well for the future. It would be released tonight and hopefully the media would leave me alone.

My lawyer was also going to remind Keith's lawyer of the undertaking which his client had signed with the court promising to leave me alone and threaten court action if he didn't comply with his undertaking. While the undertaking wasn't legally enforceable, if we asked for a protection order from the court they would look at the fact that Keith hadn't followed the undertaking he took with the court as part of the conditions of his charges. She assured me that a court would not look kindly to him refusing to follow the undertaking.

Keiran rang me after my statement was released congratulating me on finally standing up for myself. He offered to run decoy tomorrow if they media was there so I could get back to my parents place without being noticed and also offered for me to stay with him for a bit so Keith couldn't find me. I assured him my lawyer was advising his lawyer he couldn't come near me and that I would be fine. I didn't need the stress of being away from my family and I had a few orders to get done before I was taking leave to have my babies.

Keiran decided he was going to rent a place closer to me for a few months to help with the business and be close by for when the babies were due. He told me he would see me tomorrow and then would be a couple of weeks in Sydney before he organised to relocate for a few months near me. He could practically work from anywhere as long as he had his computer with him and an internet connection. After our conversation I decided to get some much needed sleep. I knew I would be up every couple of hours with the nurses taking my vitals and going to the bathroom.

Chapter 11

Keith's POV

I can't believe Cameron won't let me be with her and the babies while she is in the labour ward. I just wanted to speak to her and apologise for what had gone down but she wouldn't even give me the time of day. I know I hadn't let her explain when it first happened but I realised now I had made huge mistakes along the way and wanted to make up for those.

Keiran was allowed in and so was her family. I was furious with her for that. I called my parents and my lawyer and they had turned up. My lawyer was threatening the hospital with legal action for keeping me away from my wife. My parents wanted to know what was happening with there grandchildren as I had informed them she was having twins. My dad had expressed how he was worried for her with the stress of everything and the damage it could do to her and the twins. He also reminded me and my lawyer I had signed away all rights to the baby that Cameron was carrying. I got my lawyer onto it to see if he could have that overturned or if there was a loophole in it.

The hospital had there lawyer step in and used the paper work I had signed to keep me away from Cameron. It was a mess and all I wanted was to see my wife and find out if my children were ok. When Keiran walked out of the hospital with Phil, Cameron's brother I quickly made my way over to them.

"Keiran, how is she? How are my kids?" I asked. "Stay away from my sister. You signed those kids away remember?" Phil said. "Phil how about you go grab her some dinner and I'll meet you back here soon. I'll just get rid of my brother and parents" Keiran said. Phil nodded his head taking off to get Cameron food.

I had ordered roses and a teddy for Cameron and had written an apology to her which would be delivered shortly. The letter asked her to ring me so we could talk and I just hoped she would call. I had tried to call her when I found out what Sarah had done but her phone was disconnected and I didn't know where she was. I hired a private investigator to track her down and he did at her parents place. I got the shock of my life when I saw her heavily pregnant through her parents door. I had heard she was pregnant the night I kicked her out but I didn't know she was that far along. I knew then the baby was definitely mine and I had to get my family back at all costs.

I loved Cameron and we had planned children together but Sarah convinced me she had been cheating on me and was using me for my money. Things weren't adding up when Cameron took nothing from the house besides her business equipment, she didn't take any of the clothes I had brought her nor any jewellery, not even her wedding and engagement ring. She took no money from our joint accounts and in fact had herself removed from them. I was still angry with her and was seen with different women every week. She didn't even fight for financial support as long as I signed that I had no claim to any baby she birthed which I signed immediately. I now regretted that whole heartedly.

Sarah was always around wanting to be on my arm and eventually she had gone to the media to announce our relationship even though we weren't in any kind of relationship. Ten days ago I had someone contact me letting me know Sarah had orchestrated a plan to get rid of Cameron and take her place as my wife and he had helped by editing photos and sending messages from a computer system pretending to be from Cameron's number for money which Sarah hadn't sent through. I immediately reported it to the police who straight away started investigating it.

Two days ago they arrested Sarah and I immediately got to work on trying to get Cameron back. Problem was I had no idea where she was. I just knew I needed to apologise so things could go back to the way they were. Her lawyer wouldn't disclose her location or anything about her. I still loved Cameron and I knew she loved me. If I could just speak to her we could sort it out. I would admit to my mistakes and we could be happy again.

"Keith you need to leave. You have no right to be here and you know that. All you are doing is causing her stress which isn't good for her or the babies" my brother said snapping me out of my thoughts. "She is my wife and is carrying my children" I replied. If anything he had no right to be here. "The wife you physically hurt and tossed out.

The wife you so conveniently forgot about while you were sleeping with other woman and the children you signed away. Did you forget about that?" Keiran asked me.

"I made mistakes ok? Mistakes that I will apologise for every day of our lives. I love Cameron and we always planned to have a family" I replied. "Mistakes? No that's not a mistake and the fact you think that Cameron will just forgive you speaks volumes. You think a simple sorry will fix what you did? I was there the next morning and saw the damage you did to her and the place. You allowed our parents to publicly humiliate her and you did the same. Do you really think sorry will fix it all? She has been working her arse off to get what she needs for her children while you have been publicly disowning them now you want to claim them and so do our parents? It doesn't work like that. She has gotten this far without you. She works 10-12 hour days at her business so she will be able to have 6 weeks off after the twins are born. So don't you dare discredit what you and our parents did to her" he yelled before storming away from me.

How the hell did he know all that? I knew I needed to beg Cameron for forgiveness and I would. I would get down on my knees and bag her till she took me back. Then she could close her silly little business and be a stay at home mum and a wife.

Chapter 12

Cameron's POV

It was now 7am and I was up for the day. I had showered and changed and was sitting up in bed. I had the TV on and the news was playing. "Breaking news, we have Mr Keith Young ready to speak to us about the on going situation with his wife. Let's cross to Gemma who is with Mr Young outside the hospital his wife was admitted to yesterday" the anchor man said before they cut to the hospital I was in. "Thanks Tim. I'm here this morning with Mr Keith Young who has agreed to speak to me on camera after his wife's lawyer released a statement from Mrs Cameron Young last night. It's the first time since this begun that Cameron has spoken publicly about what has happened. Mr Young, can you confirm that what Cameron said in her statement is true? You are both separated? she made it seem like there would be no getting back together" Gemma asked before shoving the microphone into Keith's face.

"I would like to first apologise to my wife on behalf of my self and my parents for publicly humiliating her and using the media to do so. She has handled herself with dignity and grace during the entire situation. She has worked and supported herself and our children during this pregnancy without the help from myself or my family and I am eternally grateful to her for keeping our children safe. She is an amazing, strong woman and I am very proud of all she has achieved for herself and her business. While we work out our differences we both ask the media for privacy. As you can imagine it's a hard time for both myself and Cameron and we both need to think of our children. Trust has been broken and our foundations have been damaged but we will rebuild and come back stronger together. I love my wife immensely. Cameron if you are watching, I am so sorry love and I promise to make it up to you for the rest of my life" Keith said.

"Mr Young it is reported you allegedly assaulted your wife hitting her and knocking her to the ground, destroying your home while she was in the early stages of pregnancy. What do you have to say about that?" Gemma asked. "I have no comment about that. I will say though that I am extremely upset with what has transpired and hope the full arm of the law is brought down on those responsible for causing these issues between my wife and I. I apologise for my part in it all and am willing to put in the work with Cameron so we can move forward together as a family for our children" Keith responded before the interview ended.

Great just great. I had wanted everything kept out of the media and here Keith was airing it all. What was he hoping to achieve? He was speaking like this was from both of us but I had not said any of that. In fact I had no plans of working on anything but keeping my babies in my belly for a while longer then birthing them into the world.

My phone rang pulling me from my thoughts and it was my lawyer. "Hi Cameron, I have been inundated with requests for interviews and photos of you pregnant" my lawyer said. "I'm not doing any interviews. I didn't want this splashed all over the news. I have never wanted anything public" I replied. We spent over 30 minutes on the phone and came up with a statement which would be passed onto the media.

The statement was short and simple. "Cameron is still currently recovering in hospital after her scare. She has not had a single conversation with Mr Young. They remain legally separated and have been since April 2005 when she left the house they shared together. Cameron asks for privacy while she focuses on her pregnancy and thanks everyone for there well wishes". It would be released immediately to the media. I left the TV off and waited for family to turn up and for the doctor to release me. I just wanted to get home and away from the waiting media.

Soon Keiran and my family turned up. "I have security waiting for us outside to get you to your car. The media is relentless out there. Keith and my parents are in the foyer as well. I have asked them to leave but they refuse to. Your parents came through the back way and that's the way we will get you out. Having the security will draw the media that way so you can get out of here. I'll lead them away and then come see you in a couple of days when the media backs off" Keiran said. "Thanks Keiran. I owe you one" I replied. "Don't be silly, I'm protecting my nieces" he replied. We all shook our heads at him.

Dr Laine came past about 10am to check on me and the twins and was happy with my blood pressure and the twins so said I could head home but I had to rest for a week and return next week for another check up. I had orders to get through and were worried about those. My mum and dad assured me that they would get the orders done with Sage and have them sent out.

I hadn't even checked in if I had new orders come in yet. But I couldn't worry about that. I had to keep myself calm for the sake of my children now. I said goodbye to Keiran after he helped to get the flowers into my parents car and we slipped out the back away from the waiting media. I was looking forward to getting home and into a nice relaxing bath and spending the rest of the day in my pjs on the couch watching trashy TV.

Chapter 13

Cameron's POV

I fell asleep on the couch watching Dirty Dancing my all time favourite movie. "No body puts baby in the corner". Only to be woken by people talking trying to be quiet.

I looked towards the verandah where the front door was to see my mum and dad speaking with Keith and his parents. It looked to be heated but they were whisper yelling. I needed to go to the bathroom before I wet myself but that would mean everyone would know I was awake. I decided that wetting myself was worse then everyone knowing I was awake. I got up just as Keiran and Phil came up the back stairs. I waddled my way to the stairs going up to the bathroom ignoring everyone as they were now staring at me.

"Cameron, love please talk to me" Keith called out but my main concern now was not wetting my pants. I had at least one baby jumping on my bladder for god sake. I made my way to the bathroom just making it before I wet myself and then headed out. "You need to leave Keith. You are not welcome here. The doctor said no stress. It's not good for the twins. You and your parents have done enough damage" my father said. I didn't want to see any of them but clearly they were not going to listen to anyone.

"Please I just want to talk to Cameron. I need to apologise for what I have done. I know I made mistakes but it wasn't my fault" Keith begged. "It is your fault you stupid boy. You believed the wrong woman and then paraded your new flavour around week after week while my daughter worked her butt off to afford those babies she is carrying. Don't you dare blame anyone but yourself. Your own brother supported my daughter in her pregnancy after you hit her and threw her and those babies out" my mother raged. She hardly ever got angry but she was going mumma bear on these people. I wrapped my arms around my stomach feeling the need to protect my children from these people. These people did damage to both myself and my babies but vilifying us in the media.

I walked down the stairs holding my stomach. It was heavy and I found lifting it helped to take some pressure off my joints. "You all need to leave. None of you are welcome here and none of you besides Keiran are welcome around my children" I spoke. "Cameron please" Keith started. "No, none of you stopped to listen to me so I have no problems doing the same. You made your decision and I have made mine. Get out, leave" I spat out.

"Cam, are you ok?" Keiran asked noticing me lifting my stomach. "Umm it's just heavy, I need a support band. I'll get one in a couple of weeks" I replied dismissing him. "Why aren't you getting one now?" Keith asked. "It's none of your god damn business Keith" I replied before continuing, "if you must know I have other expenses I need to pay this month so back off" I replied.

"Cam, you could give birth in a few weeks why didn't you tell me?" Phil said. "Phil it's fine, I had other things to buy for the twins and it can wait. Plenty of pregnant women don't use them" I replied. "Plenty of pregnant women aren't working 12 hour days on there feet, lifting heavy equipment" Keiran replied.

I just glared at him. I didn't have anyone but myself to rely on and I'd be damned if some trust fund baby tried to make me feel bad for supporting myself and my children. "Sorry Cameron. I just want what's best for my nieces" he said after noticing me glaring. "My grand babies are girls? Oh I can't wait to get them matching dresses and show them off" my ex mother in law Maz stated. "You won't be doing anything with my children. You will not be anywhere near them" I replied. "We are having girls? Cameron? We are having baby girls?" Keith said in a state of shock. "I don't know the gender of my children. There is no we Keith, you made sure of that remember. I think it is best you all leave now" I said before heading back to the couch. My back was starting to hurt and I didn't want my contractions to start again.

Mum, dad, Phil and Keiran came into the house locking the others out. "Can someone grab me some water please" I asked. "Love please. I just want to talk to you. I'm sorry for everything. Please love open the door. I'll send my parents away so we can talk. I'm so sorry. I should of let you explain. I should of never believed Sarah. I love you Cameron. Please tell me what to do to fix this. I'm down on my knees begging you to forgive me. Love please tell me what to do" Keith called through the door. "Go home Keith, there is nothing you can do. We are over, you put your hands on me in anger to hurt me. You have slept with countless women and you disowned your own flesh and blood and for what?" I replied.

"Please love we can work it out. I'm sorry baby so very sorry. Those women meant nothing to me. I swear, they were just a distraction to try and forget you" Keith called out. "You think that's the worst thing you did? No sleeping with them I don't care about. You and your parents disowned my children and called them every name under the sun. You publicly spoke of them being nothing but bastard children who I was using for your money. How do you think they will feel when they are older and that's still out there on the web for them to see? Nothing you or your parents say or do will change what you have said about my children. Remember that Keith. You signed away your own children. Please just leave this isn't healthy for me or the twins" I replied before breaking down in tears. I couldn't do this now, I needed to be strong for my babies and I needed him out of my life again so I could move on with mine.

Chapter 14

Keith's POV

I am currently arguing with my in laws about letting me into the house so I can talk to Cameron. I can see her sleeping on the couch and there is nothing more than I want to be doing than to be sitting there stroking her belly that holds my babies. My lawyer is working on a way to get the paper work dismissed where I signed away my rights. I did that in anger when I thought she had cheated on me. My brother had never once believed that my wife had cheated on me and I found out he had been supporting her the entire time. I was angry with him on the one hand but then I was thankful someone else was looking out for her while I was off doing other things which I now regret.

I look up to see Cameron making her way upstairs again she is ignoring me as I try to reason with her. I want nothing more than to barge into that house and embrace my wife begging her for forgiveness but these are her parents in front of me and I can't. She comes out of the bathroom and heads back downstairs telling me and my parents to leave but my brother asks if she is ok because she is holding her stomach. When she bites back at me because of me asking about her why she isn't buying a support band speaking about having other expenses I realised how much I fucked up. Cameron was never after my money and I should of seen that sooner. She never once took anything from our joint account even when we were together.

I don't know how to get her to speak to me at all. She won't even look at me let alone talk to me. The woman I love literally wants nothing to do with me and it's my own fault. I send my parents to the car hoping that Cameron will want to just speak with me. "Cameron it's just me now. Please just come out and speak to me then I will go if you want me to" I call through the door. I watch as she struggles to get off the couch hitting away her brother and my brothers hands when they offer to help. That should be me helping her up right now. I have missed out on her entire pregnancy but I don't plan on missing out on anything else. I just need to get her to forgive me.

Cameron makes her way outside and sits on the church pew which was next to the front door on the verandah. "You have 5 minutes. This isn't good for the babies" Cameron said. I sat down next to her and went to take her hand which she refused pulling her hand away.

I sigh " I'm so sorry love. I wasn't thinking and Sarah got under my skin. She had someone use a computer program to make photos of you with another man and to send text messages and emails from your phone. I should of known it wasn't true. I'll do anything to make this right Cameron. Please just tell me what to do" I said to her. I needed her in my life and would do anything she asked.

"Keith, you hit me for Christ sake. You moved on with other women. Please just let me do the same. You have already signed away your rights to these babies. Find someone else start fresh. I don't want to be in the spotlight with everyone wondering if I am just back with you for money. I don't want to be reminded daily of everything you and your family did to me. If the woman you slept with when you threw away our marriage were in our house, our bed or coming back any time soon. I want my kids to grow up away from all of that. They deserve to live without the scandal that you and your parents caused. I'm doing well here. I have my business and the support of my parents. Your life is in Sydney" Cameron states. She has already given up on me.

"Please baby, you sound like it is already over. Tell me how to fix this and I will" I reply. "That's the thing Keith. You can't fix it. You can't even acknowledge that you hit me let alone what you and your parents did. The only one who supported me and helped me is Keiran. Not once did he use the media to vilify me. Not once did he speak about me to the media even though he has known where I was from the beginning. In fact he helped get me out of Sydney when you threaten me. Don't you see Keith? I'm not what you want or need anymore. I'm just a pregnant woman with a business to run from a small town. You even said yourself, you belong with someone like Sarah" Cameron said.

I dropped down to my knees in front of Cameron looking into her eyes. Those eyes that I fell in love with "I'm begging you baby please give me another chance. I'll get help I swear. I will never ever raise my hand to you again. I am so sorry and I will spend the rest of my life telling you that every day. If you never want to see my parents again I will do that. I'm begging you Cameron please give me a chance" I say. I am almost in tears, I treated this woman like trash and she hasn't once come out and said anything against me.

I knew I had been wrong and I needed her to see I was going to be better for her and our babies. "Your 5 minutes are up Keith. Please for the sake of my babies, go home. I need to remain calm. The stress isn't good and you and your parents are bringing me stress. I don't want the media to find me so please go back to Sydney" Cameron says before trying to stand up. I try to help but she won't let me.

"Keiran can you please help?" she calls out and my brother comes out helping her up. "Go home Keith" she says before she walks inside. "Keith you owe her this much. You hurt her a lot and she just wants to focus on her pregnancy and getting her business in a great position so she can take a few weeks off once the babies are born. Take our parents and go, you all caused more than enough damage" Keiran says before he goes inside.

"Fuck. I promise you Cameron I'm not going to give up on you or our twins" I call out before heading out to the car. I would take my parents home and then come back to win my wife back and get my family that I so desperately wanted to be part of.

Chapter 15

Cameron's POV

It's been a week of me resting at home. I had to close my orders because I was now a week behind and that meant losing money. I had spoken with Keiran every day, he had gone back to Sydney so the media wouldn't get wind of where I was. He was staying away to protect my location. I also hadn't heard from Keith which was just fine by me. He had been in the media several times during the week apologising publicly to me and asking for privacy while we healed as a family. Bitch didn't realise he wasn't in my family anymore.

I was up early today because I could go back to work. I was 31 weeks pregnant and needed to finish as many of my orders as I could because I could literally go into labour at any point. Sage wasn't working for the next couple of weeks because she was sitting her HSC at the moment so I was behind in orders and working alone.

Just after 6.30am I took off to my office to start the day. Phil wasn't impressed seeing me pull up so early, he and the guys opened the garage at 7 but got there at 6.30 to have breakfast together. I just waved and headed into my work switching everything on and opening the windows. It was a bit stuffy in here from being locked up for a week. My brother popped his head in "Cameron, I brought you some breakfast over, I'm guessing you didn't eat before coming here. You should still be taking it easy" Phil scolded me. "Yes mum" I replied rolling my eyes at him. I was pregnant for Christ sake not sick or fragile.

Phil left the food saying he would be back to check on me soon and that I had better of eaten otherwise he would call Keiran. There isn't much Keiran could do cause he was back in Sydney. I got to work printing the first lot of orders then worked on the computer looking at what I had missed in the week I was off and reordering inks and stock that I would need for my other orders.

The printing equipment beeped which indicated that job was done. I cleared the equipment cleaning it up and hung up the prints I had just done to set before resetting up the next order to go. I prepared the tie dye things and got to work. Before I knew it the next large order was ready to hang, I had gotten through half the tie dye stuff I had to do today and Phil was back for lunch scolding me for not eating breakfast. I packed the first order I had done because it was ready for postage while I took bites of the sandwich with Phil watching me like a hawk. I was in a sports bra and some Kmart tights. I also had on a belly support band that Keiran had sent me which helped take the pressure off for a while. My feet were swollen but I was a busy woman with work to do. Phil left after I had eaten and I got back to work.

About 4pm someone came into my work space but I was to busy to look up. I had to finish this tie dye so it would dry overnight and then be washed and dried again to send out. I had printed 2 massive orders and they needed to be packed and sent out along with several of the smaller orders. I was trying to fit 2.5 days worth of work into 1 so I could reopen my orders. I would be here tonight till at least 11 so I could pack the orders I had done today for postage but I didn't care at this point. I just had to do it.

"Cameron have you stopped at all today?" Keiran asked me. I looked up seeing him and smiled. Phil came walking in to "she hasn't stopped but I did make her eat a sandwich for lunch" he told Keiran. I stuck my tongue out at Phil "taddle tail" I said before going back to what I was doing. "Oh and Phil get out, I don't need grease on my work" I called. "I'm going home to shower but I'm coming straight back to help you. I doubt you will be leaving it any time soon" he replied before taking off.

"Cameron put me to work. You can't do this alone. You will go into labour early if you keep working like this" Keiran said. "I'm fine Keiran. I need to get these done. I'm a week behind and had to shut my orders so I could catch up" I replied. Keiran came over and grabbed my shoulders. "Cameron I'm not asking. This is for my nieces or nephews. Let me help please?" He asked.

It was the first time he acknowledged that I might be having anything other than girls so I knew he was being serious. I nodded and set him up printing the labels to send out the orders I had managed to get done and putting them on the satchels and packing the orders. I also made him write little thank you notes apologising for the delay. Phil came back and he and Keiran got the orders I had finished packed up and ready to be picked up in the morning. I was finished by 9pm and I was utterly exhausted. I wished I had a bed at my office cause I would literally just fall into it now.

"Cameron, I'm driving you home. You look shattered and I won't allow you to drive" Phil said. "No Phil I need my car to get back here early again" I replied. "Cameron you can't keep doing this to you or the babies. You should be resting" Phil replied. "Phil it's just me. I have no one else to rely on to pay my bills. This is for me and my babies so I can take some time off when they arrive. Don't start on me and try to guilt me into slowing down. I don't have a choice in the matter" I replied. "Cam, I'll pick you up at 7 and bring you back if you let Phil drive you home now" Keiran said. "Yeh and how are you going to do that?" I asked. "I'm staying at Moby's" Keiran replied. "Ok fine but if you are later than 7 I will walk here" I replied. Both Phil and Keiran agreed and I was lead to Phil's car and driven home. I fell into a deep sleep that night.

Chapter 16

Cameron's POV

The next morning I was up and ready by 7am. When I opened the blinds at the glass doors, I saw the verandah was covered in bunches of flowers and balloons. I stepped out picking up the card reading it

My Dearest Cameron,No words can express how sorry I truely am. Let's start again for our babies sake. Please go on a date with me tonight?Love your husbandKeith

Great just great. Now I have to clean this up before heading to work. Keiran came walking up the stairs just as the home phone rang. I ran, well waddled quickly, to answer it seeing my mum and dad weren't up yet.

"Hello" I said. "Cameron love, did you get my delivery?" Keith asked. "Yes Keith, I got the flowers. You shouldn't have wasted your money" I started only to be interrupted by Keith. "It's not a waste of my money for you love. So what is your answer?" He asked. "Keith I'm swamped with orders. I don't have time for this" I said before saying "I have to go to work. Please leave me be Keith. Flowers are not going to change a thing". I hung up the phone to see mum and dad looking at the verandah. "Sorry" I said. Mum waved me off saying she would take care of it and sent me off to work with Keiran driving me.

This went on for another two week, different gifts arriving every morning and phone calls morning and night to my parents phone from Keith. Keiran stayed at Moby's helping me with my orders during the day and setting up a better more user friendly website. He also set it up so it was more mainstream for me and I wasn't having to do things manually which I was grateful for. It cut about 20 minutes of work off every order which didn't seem a lot but it all added up and meant I could get things done more quickly. Sage was back helping now her exams were over and I had opened up my ordering system again.

One afternoon I was working with Keiran, Sage was on her break and Phil was bringing lunch over for me and Keiran when I heard someone walk into my work space. "Phil we will be out in a minute I don't need grease on my stock" I called out. I got no answer so I looked up seeing Keith standing there. "What are you doing here?" I asked. "I came to see why my wife had no time for me" he replied. "We are separated Keith remember? I will be filing the divorce papers as soon as I can" I replied. "Cameron you don't mean that" he said. "Actually I do" I replied.

I was frustrated and he didn't seem to understand flowers and gifts weren't going to fix what he had done. "Cameron I have said I was sorry. What more do you want?" He asked seeming to get angry stepping towards me. My gut feeling was to run. I didn't trust him not to hurt me. He may have only hit me once but once was enough to make me not trust him at all.

I stepped back trying to create distance between us. "Cameron you need to stop this. You are my wife, you are carrying my children. You need to shut this little set up you call a business and come home where you belong. I explained it was a mistake" he ranted. "Keith have you been drinking?" I asked. "I mean it Cameron. You are embarrassing me and my parents with this little joke of a business. You belong at home. You are bringing the next Young generation into the world. This is beneath them" he said swinging his arms around my business like it meant nothing.

"Keith get out. You aren't welcome here at all. This is my business and I won't be going anywhere with you at all. We are legally separated and you signed away your rights to these babies. You are embarrassing yourself by thinking your money will get me to ever come back to you" I replied. I was so angry that he was dismissing me, my business and what he had done. Keith stormed towards me slapping my face again which caused me to fall onto the desk beside me. I luckily used my arms to prevent me hitting my stomach. I stood up to see Keiran and Phil holding Keith back. I held my cheek "get out now" I said. "You will regret this Cameron, I will take your children from you. Mark my words. You will be begging me to take you back by the end of the week" Keith fumed before he stormed out of my business.

I sat down in the seat and began to sob. How could the man who claimed to love me and want me back think it was ok to hit me again? I was 33 weeks pregnant with his children and he had no problems lashing out at me and yet expected me to run back to him? What if he did that to the babies when he was angry at them? Phil and Keiran came over to check on me and begged me to call the police which I agreed to. Phil called mum who was going to come over before he got the footage up for the police. I called my lawyer who advised me to send a copy of the footage over to her as well.

A few hours later I was home still in shock. I had given me statement to police and they had filed charges issuing a warrant for Keith's arrest. Keiran and Phil had also given statements to the police as they had seen the entire thing happen. The TV was on in the background and breaking news bulletin came on. "Breaking news. Keith Young has been arrested and allegedly charged with assaulting his wife Cameron Young today in her place of business. She is currently in her last stages of pregnancy with the couples twins. The two have been separated since April of this year. If this is what Mr Young does while his wife is pregnant no wonder they are separated. We have no news on how Mrs Young is but we will keep you posted on this breaking news". I turned the TV off. I didn't want this all to be public, that would mean when my children were older they could see all this.

Chapter 17

Cameron's POV

It had been a week since Keith had been arrested and my business phone line had been blowing up with requests for statements and interviews from the media. I had had to release another statement through my lawyer expressing my desire for privacy for myself and the twins.

I hadn't heard from Keith thanks to the protection order that was in place. I had been working still and Keiran was doing his work from my office so he could make sure I wasn't working to hard. He also would help out when he finished his work. We worked well together and he never once put me down for "my little business" in fact he encouraged me and supported me like no other. I was working on a new design playing around with different settings on the printing machine when my private mobile rang.

I turned the printer off and answered it seeing it was my lawyer calling. "Cameron speaking" I answered. My lawyer went straight to business mode. "Cameron, Keith is going for custody of one of the twins" she said. "What? He signed away his rights?" I replied. "He is saying he signed away rights for one baby not two. He is claiming that you each have a right to raise one of the children and has filed with the federal court claiming you can't afford to raise both children. He is being supported by his parents. I have sent the paper work through to your email" she said. "Hold on I'll pull it up" I said before opening my email and seeing it.

I opened the email skimming through the paper work. "How can he do this?" I asked. Keiran was behind me reading over my shoulder. "Cameron it's going to get nasty and it's going to be costly. I can represent you but I will need a higher retainer. The bill could run into the hundred thousands" my lawyer said. "I can't afford that" I replied. "Cameron you need to give me directions, you have your first hearing in January" my lawyer said. "I will get the money. Do what needs to be done. So do I have to appear? I could be in labour then" I replied. "I'll see if I can get it adjourned. Get me paper work from your doctor informing me of the due date and get them to say it's risky for you to be that far away from the hospital. Cameron you need to know this is going to be a long hard fight. I'm sorry. I'll be in touch" my lawyer said before hanging up.

I couldn't help it, I burst into tears screaming. How could he do this? How could he try to take one of my children from me? I had never hated anyone in my life but I hated my husband for what he was doing to me and my children. I almost fell off the chair but Keiran held me and Phil and a few other mechanics came running. "Cam what's wrong? Are the babies ok?" Phil rushed out panicking. I couldn't answer him, I could barely get my breath through my sobs.

"He is going after one of the twins claiming she can't afford to raise both" Keiran answered. He was still supporting my weight because I couldn't do it myself.

Phil came round the table "I got you Cam, we will sort it. He can't do this" Phil said. "I swear Cameron I won't let my brother or my parents get away with this" Keiran said. I couldn't focus at all, as stupid as this sounded I wanted my mum, I wanted her to make it all better but I knew she couldn't, no one could. Keith was doing this just to punish me so I would go back to him. "I have to go back to him. I have to keep my babies safe" I responded. "No Cameron, that's exactly what he wants. We will fight this together" Keiran responded. "I can't afford to go against him and your parents Keiran" I replied. I was shaking by now because I was in shock. "Let's get you home Cam" Phil said before leading me out to Keiran's car, it was to hard to climb into the Ute now I was 34 weeks pregnant.

Once we got to mums place she was shocked to see us all. Keiran must of printed out the papers because he handed a copy to my mum who began reading it. Phil and Keiran lead me to the couch sitting me down. Keiran excused himself to make some phone calls while I sat looking at the black screen of the tv.

About an hour later dad came flying up the stairs, "where is she? Oh sweetheart we will be with you every step of the way. He won't take away one of the twins. You hear me?" My dad said and I couldn't help it. I burst into tears again in my dads arms. Why couldn't he just leave us alone? This was all about power and control, and because I wouldn't take him back he was punishing me by hurting my children and he wanted to do that by separating my babies. He was truely a monster. The fact the court was entertaining this was mind boggling. How could a court which was supposedly there to protect children, think this was acceptable to seperate twins because one parent wanted one baby?

Keiran came back on "I paid the retainer to your lawyer" he calmly stated. "What? Keiran I can't let you do that" I replied. "Cameron what he is doing is wrong and I won't let them take either one of those babies" he replied. "I'll pay you back. I'll sell the business and repay you as soon as I can" I replied. "No Cameron, that is just as much your baby as those babies you are carrying" Keiran replied. "We will mortgage the house" dad said. "It's covered please, it's the least I could do after what my family has done to you Cameron" Keiran stated before his phone rang. Keiran excused himself again to answer his phone just as Phil turned the TV on. "Breaking news. Keith Young has been in a motor vehicle accident. It's alleged he was drink driving and lost control of the car. Stay tuned for more details as they arise". I got up walking out to where Keiran was on the phone looking like he had seen a ghost. He swung around after hanging up the phone. "He's dead" he said before he broke down in tears. I quickly pulled him into a hug, Keith Young was dead.

Chapter 18

Cameron's POV

Keiran pulled away after breaking down in my arms. No matter what Keith did, he was still Keiran's brother and my husband, the man I loved once and the father of my unborn children. "Keiran I am so sorry" I stated. "I need to get to Sydney to be with my parents. I have to go" Keiran said. "You can't drive in that state. I'm coming with you. Just let me pack a bag ok?" I asked. Keiran just nodded his head.

I walked inside heading up to my room. "What's going on?" Phil asked. "Keith is dead. I'm driving Keiran to Sydney. Oh god, he is dead. What did I do?" I said. "What? You didn't do anything Cameron. Don't you dare blame yourself. This is all his doing. You are not driving. I'll drive the both of you and get the bus back tomorrow" Phil said. I nodded my head and go to my room to pack a weeks worth of clothes. Keiran has been there for me and now it's my turn to repay the favour, he needs me and I plan on being there for him. It took me about 20 minutes to have everything packed including my body mate pillow.

We headed to Keiran's car packing our things in the boot and Phil getting in the drivers seat. Mum and dad would be coming down for the funeral whenever that was and I would return home after that. We said our goodbyes and I hopped into the back seat to try and get comfortable for the long drive ahead. Keiran hoped in the back with me letting me rest on him and also seeking comfort. He had just lost his big brother no matter what had gone on, it was still a loss.

I must of fell asleep on the drive because I was being woken up by Phil. I was laying in Keiran's arms and he was snoring lightly. We were at the Tuggerah twin servos which was the last service station along the freeway before we hit Sydney. I knew I needed to use the bathroom and grab some food because I hadn't eaten and was starving. I sat up waking Keiran in the process with my groaning.

"Sorry, we are just stopping for a bathroom break and I'm going to grab some food. Do you want anything?" I asked. Keiran didn't respond. I tried to bend down to grab my slip on shoes but couldn't. I needed my shoes cause I was walking into the bathroom. Keiran saw and got himself out of the car coming around to my side opening my door. He helped put my shoes on and helped me get out of the car walking me across the petrol station. Phil was filling the car with petrol.

I headed into the bathroom then grabbed a heap of snacks for everyone and some water and of cause my chocolate milk. I walked outside and Keiran was waiting for me and helped me back to the car helping me in. I was still sitting in the back this time though Keiran got into the front next to Phil. We still had about 2 hours drive ahead of us until we reached Keiran's parents place. I passed out the drinks and some snacks before we headed out to finish the drive. Keiran had been on the phone several times talking to different people.

We soon reached Keiran's parents place and the media was out front of the gates with security stopping anyone from entering. When they saw Keiran's car they let us through closing the gates behind us. Keiran told Phil to park in the garage so we could get out of the car without being seen. When the garage was closed we exited the car heading into my ex in laws place.

Keiran entered first followed by Phil and I. His parents were sitting there and looked a right mess. Keiran greeted his mother then his father before his mother spotted us. "What the hell is that gold digger doing here?" She screamed. Phil stood in front of me trying to shield me. "Phil it's fine she is just hurting" I stated. "You aren't welcome here this is all your fault. I will make sure you get nothing from Keith's estate and I will take those babies from you. They are my sons children and someone like you doesn't deserve anything from us" she screamed. "Maz, I'm so sorry for your loss. I'm here only to support Keiran. I never meant to upset you. We will go. Again Max and Maz and I so very sorry for your loss. No parent should have to bury a child" I stated. "You bitch, this is your fault. You caused my son to die and then you come into my home. I will destroy you and take those children" Maz screamed out.

"Mum knock it off. She did nothing. If anything it is your fault for enabling Keith to do what he wanted without consequences. He choose to get into his car drunk. Cameron had nothing to do with it at all. If you don't stop this now you will lose me as well" Keiran said coming to my defence. "Keiran it's fine. We will go. I'll let you know where I am staying. If you need anything day or night please just call" I replied.

"Going after my other son now? You are nothing but a gold digger. You won't get a cent from us" Maz spat. "Look Maz, I can't say I know the pain you are in but I don't want a cent from any of you and never have" I replied. I was getting annoyed, not once had I even thought about money. All I wanted to do was support Keiran and be there for him like he had been there for me my entire pregnancy. He was my friend and needed someone while he mourned his brother who just happened to be a man I was married too.

"Get out. You are nothing but trash" Maz screamed. I nodded heading to the car to get my things before I called a cab. "I warned you mum. I'm sorry dad but I can't be around her. Please let me know arrangements for the funeral. I'm taking Cameron to my place" Keiran said before we all headed back to his car and driving over to his place without another word being said.

Chapter 19

Cameron's POV

Phil left the next morning early to jump on the bus back to Forster where dad would pick him up. He would return with my parents for the funeral to support Keiran and myself. I honestly was numb. I didn't know how to feel about it all. He was the man I loved once upon a time but he had hurt me and part of me was relieved I wouldn't have to fight in court for my babies. I felt guilty for thinking that as well. I was also sad, he was the father of my children and as much as he had hurt me, my children lay of wanted to know him one day.

My lawyer had been in touch stating the police had a letter for me from Keith. Turns out Keith had got into his car drunk on purpose and rammed into a wall. He was alive when the paramedics got to him but died on route to the hospital. Keiran had spent most of the morning on the phone with his dad planning the funeral and organising the memorial. He asked if I wanted to speak at the service but I declined. I had nothing to really say. I also didn't want to be in the spotlight. Maz had been in the media this morning claiming I was attempting to take all of Keith's estate but that was news to me. I had no intention of claiming anything from Keith, we weren't together when he took his own life.

A knock on the door brought me out of my thoughts and soon his mum and dad were storming into Keiran's lounge room. "You" Maz screamed at me. I stood up not liking the look in her eyes. Keiran noticed and put himself between us. "I swear if you don't disappear I will make you. Sarah may not of been able to get rid of you but I sure as hell will and take your children" Maz screamed. "What?" I replied. "You think I didn't have a hand in getting rid of you? You just had to get in Keiran's head though. You were never good enough for Keith and you deserved everything you got. It's a shame that he worked out what I had done yesterday" she yelled before she realised what she had said. "Maz what the hell did you do?" Max screamed.

My phone dinged and it was a copy of the letter coming through that my lawyer sent.

My dearest Cameron,What did I do to deserve an angel like you? I loved you with my whole heart and then I lost you which is my biggest regret. I'm so sorry for allowing my mum to hurt you and our beautiful children. I found out she and Sarah were working together to get rid of you. I should of known but was blinded by rage and for that I am eternally sorry. She was going to take our babies from me and threatened to cut me off if I didn't agree to take custody of our children. I couldn't allow it, I didn't want them growing up like me. I'm sorry I wasn't strong enough to stand up to her. I know this is the cowards way out, but I'm doing this for you and our children. Please know I never stopped loving you at all. I want you and our twins to be happy and live a life full of love and laughs. Please tell them how much there dad loved them. My dearest Cameron please find a man who loves you as much as I do and be happy. Keep our children safe from my mother. Love Keith.

I gasped and tried to stop myself crying. I had blocked out what was happening around me. "You, you pushed him to take his life? You pushed him to take my children and you forced him to go for custody threatening to take everything from him? How could you do that? How could you hurt your own child?" I asked. Maz shoved Keiran out of the way storming towards me looking like she was ready to kill. Maz raised her foot looking like she was going to kick me but was tackled by Max. I was to shocked to move. Keiran wrapped his arm around me leading me to his room before he called the police.

Within the hour Maz had been arrested and I was in a state of shock. Keiran and Max were trying to talk to me but I couldn't respond. It was like I wasn't there. Max sent for a doctor to come check me out while Keiran helped me into bed putting me under the blankets because I was shaking. How could a mother do that to her own child? How could someone try to harm unborn children that she professed to love because it was the last connection to her son? I had to many thoughts in my head and I started to feel sick. "Help me up" I called before Max and Keiran helped me up. I waddled my way to the bathroom just in time to empty my stomach into the toilet. My knees gave out and I was on the floor with Keiran and Max shouting something.

Next moment I woke in a hospital bed connected to different machines and had an IV pumping fluid into me. I looked around the room noticing the twins heartbeats were being monitor and they looked stable. I was also hooked up to a heart monitor. In the corner Keiran was sleeping on a couch. "Keiran" I called. He shot up quickly looking at me. "You're awake? I'll grab the doctor". He said before exiting the room.

Keiran walked back in a few minutes later with a woman I have never seen before. "Hi I'm Jenny one of the midwives here tonight. How are you feeling?" She asked. "Im ok. What happened?" I asked. "Well you fainted" she replied. I nodded my head in understanding. "The doctor will be here shortly but you will be spending the night with us. We spoke to your midwife team already and let them know what happened. Your babies are stable for now. Try to get some more rest ok?" She said. I just nodded again and she was gone. "Keiran, what happened?" I asked. "You fainted after my mother tried to attack you. I'm so sorry Cameron" he said. "It's not your fault we are ok" I replied. He just nodded his head.

The doctor soon came in repeating what the midwife had said. He let me know he had put me on blood pressure medication which I would need to stay on for the rest of my pregnancy and informed me I needed to rest as much as possible. He also let me know if my blood pressure remained stable overnight he would send me home in the morning. He gave me his condolences and left. "Do you mind if I stay with you the night?" Keiran asked. "Not at all. We will be ok if you want to head home though" I replied. He just waved me off and got back on the couch. We both dozed off pretty quickly.

Chapter 20

Cameron's POV

Today was the day of the funeral. My parents and Phil had arrived early and were with me at Keiran's place. Max was also here and had been staying in one of the guest rooms. He had no idea what his wife had done and didn't want to be around her. He was extremely remorseful to me. I waved him off not wanting to dwell on the past. I needed to keep calm and focus on the future for myself and my children, nothing else mattered.

Maz had been charged as well and would be heading to court in the new year with Sarah. Max didn't want to return to his wife at all and had begun proceedings to seperate from her legally. She was a bitter, twisted woman who had in fact destroyed her entire family.

The funeral cars would be picking up Max and Keiran. They had tried to convince me to go with them but I didn't want to be front and centre for the media. I would be there to support both of them but I wanted to stay in the background. My parents, Phil and I left early to be in the church prior to the Young's arriving. When we pulled up to the church, the media was already waiting. I grabbed the black umbrellas my parents had brought and opened my door opening the umbrella blocking myself from the waiting media. Phil helped me out of the car using his body as a shield. Security came to surround me as well which Keiran must of organised.

Reporters were calling out questions to me but I refused to acknowledge any of them. I walked into the church and took my seat with my parents and brother. I had people coming up to me trying to talk and offer there condolences and congratulations for the pregnancy but the security kept them away. I knew these people were all fake, I had learnt that the hard way. I was here to support Max and Keiran only.

Maz walked in by herself and looked a right mess. Everyone avoided her like the plaque. She looked towards me and came storming over. The media in the back of the church was watching on ready for the drama to televise it to the world. Phil and dad shot up out of there seats and the security acted quickly stopping her from coming closer. Mum grabbed onto my hands squeezing it for support.

"You gold digging whore how dare you come to my sons funeral causing a scene. You just want his money and I will make sure you never see a cent neither will those bastards you are carrying" she screamed. I didn't respond at all and focused on the front of the church. "Don't you ignore me you bitch. My son would be alive if you had of just disappeared like I planned" she called. I stood up "I'm so sorry you are hurting Maz. No parent should feel the loss of one of there children. I think you should take your seat" I replied. She went to lunge for me and security grabbed her walking her out of the church. I sat back down with everyone staring at me including the media. "Please we are here to celebrate the life of Keith Young. Let's show him and his family the respect they deserve during this hard time" I called out. Everyone turned away from me so we could get the funeral started.

I had purposely stayed back from the family section of the church sitting behind where they would sit so I could still offer support to Max and Keiran but not be the centre of attention. The coffin was brought in followed by Max and Keiran who both stopped next to where I was sitting. Keiran extended his hand to me and I slightly shook my head. He nodded his head and then Max also came over. Phil helped me stand and I took Keiran and Max's hand. They took me to the front seat sitting me between both of them. Both of them gripped my hands through the service. The twins were going ballistic in my stomach so I placed both Max's and Keiran's hand on my stomach allowing them to feel the babies moving hoping it offered some form of comfort. A part of Keith was still around and always would be in Max and Keiran's life.

After Keiran and Max both spoke it was time for the coffin to be walked out to the waiting car and taken to the crematorium. Both Max and Keiran were going to be helping to carry the coffin along with 2 of Keith's friends. The priest asked for two volunteers and my father and Phil both stood up walking over to the coffin. They stood side by side with the others carrying the coffin out of the church. The priest came towards me helping me stand and then we began to walk out of the church.

My mum rushed to my side holding my arm as we walked out. Many of my so called friends tried to do the same however were stopped by security who were following me. The cameras were flashing as I made my way out of the church. I headed over to Keiran and Max who both embraced me and my family. Keiran was sobbing on my shoulder and asked me to accompany them to the crematorium which was for family only. I nodded my head, I knew he needed my support. I let me parents know what was happening and they said they would follow behind us.

When we arrived at the crematorium, my brother and father again helped to lift the coffin into the chapel. There was no media here at all. It was private will all of 20 people who had been close to Keith or his family. We followed the coffin in and stood around in while the priest said a few words and a pray was said. The curtains soon closed and it all came to an end. Just like that Keith Young was just a memory to everyone.

I walked outside the chapel and finally allowed myself to break down. That man had once been my entire world. I did still love him in a way. I also felt for him, how bad was his life to just throw it away to protect me and my babies? Max, Keiran and my family surrounded me holding me up as I sobbed for what could of been. I don't remember much else but I remember Keiran kissing my forehead and telling me he would be there for the birth of my babies and would see me soon. I also remember being put into my parents car but most of it was a blur.

Chapter 21

Cameron's POV

I was currently 36 weeks and 6 days pregnant back home with my parents. I had spoken to Keiran every day checking on him and him asking about the babies. He had stayed in Sydney to be close to his dad and sort out Keith's estate. Keiran assured me I would be getting the majority of it but I really didn't want it. I felt I didn't deserve it, we were separated when he passed. Keiran wouldn't have it saying the twins were the ones who would benefit from it as they grew up. I didn't argue with him but I didn't help either. Whatever would be would be. Maz was fighting them all the way anyway and I didn't need the added stress of it all.

I was still working in my business and it was going well. Sage was working full time now and was a god send. I would do the paper work and the printing of labels while she did the making and filling the orders. I also employed two other girls to help her and was training them for when the babies arrived. They were school kids and worked 2 afternoons a week and alternate Saturdays.

I had come home early today, I was extra irritable and snappy. I was uncomfortable and ready for the babies to come. It was summer and hot and I couldn't get comfortable no matter what. I had ignored the call from Keiran this afternoon just wanting to get some sleep seeing I hadn't slept properly the night before. I went to bed early promising myself I would call Keiran in the morning to apologise for ignoring him today.

I was asleep pretty quickly but woke just after midnight busting to go to the toilet. As I stood up out of bed my water broke. "Mum, come quick. My water just broke" I called out. "You probably just wet yourself Cameron go back to bed" mum called back. "Mum it's still coming. My water just broke" I called back. My mum and dad came running into the room. "Shit" dad said. "We need to call the midwife" mum said.

I rang my midwife and Jane answered telling me it was time to come in. I also called Keiran who answered when I called the second time. "Cameron it's 1 in the morning, I'll talk to you tomorrow" he said. "Keiran my water broke. I'm going to shower and head into the hospital. I thought you might want to know" I said. "What? The babies are coming. Shit stay calm Cameron ok just stay calm, shit" Keiran rambled. "Hey Keiran, I think you need to calm down. Wake your dad and let him know and then if you want to make your way to John Hunter, I will meet you there" I said trying not to laugh at him. "Ok stay calm Cameron, ok" Keiran continued to ramble. "Keiran. I think you need to wake your dad and stay calm. Drive safely please" I said before hanging up.

I headed up to the shower and took a quick shower washing my hair. I didn't know when I would get a shower next and wanted to be clean. Dad and Phil packed the car up with my bags, my pillow and snacks. We would be taking two cars. Mine because they had the car seats and my parents so I could lay in the back while we drove to John Hunter. Phil was going to be driving my car and dad was driving my parents car with me in the back. We headed to the car to make our way to the hospital. I still hadn't had any contractions at this point and was really excited to be close to meeting my babies. I noted the date which was January 21st 2006 and sat comfortably in the car. The contractions hit while on the way but they were manageable.

We got to John hunter and I was signed in before being taken to a room by Jane to check how I was progressing. Phil waited outside for Keiran and Max to arrive because he didn't want to see anything. Jane checked my progress and I was 3cm dilated and the babies heart rate was strong and stable. Jane said I was free to move around as much as I wanted. I couldn't have a water birth though as the pool was being used by another mother. I could however use the shower and bath tub while I laboured. Jane was going to stay with me throughout the labour. I could have whoever I wanted with me in the room.

Keiran and Max arrived about an hour after we did and came into the room. Keiran sat next to me while I was rocking on the birthing ball and put pressure on my lower back which is where most of my contractions were. Jane also used heat packs helping with the pain.

I laboured for 12 hours naturally and was progressing slowly. I was 6cms dilated but all of a sudden the babies heart rates dropped. Jane was calling for the doctor immediately while trying to get me on the bed. I was panicking and didn't know what was wrong. I was laid on my left side with my parents, Keiran and Max trying to assure me everything was going to be ok.

Phil had slept through the entire thing. Dr Laine came in and checked on me and the babies. "Cameron your babies are in distress and we need to get them out quickly. We want to do a C-section as you aren't fully dilated yet" he said. I quickly agreed and soon they were rushing me towards the operating theatre with Keiran following behind. They set up for an epidural while Dr Laine went through everything that could go wrong. I couldn't focus on anything and grabbed hold of Keiran's hand. "I'm right here Cam, I got you" he said.

I was sat on the side of the bed and the anaesthesiologist set up to administer an epidural, the entire time Keiran held onto my hand telling me everything was going to be ok. Once it was administered I was laid down on the bed and the doctors quickly got to work preparing for the emergency c section. Keiran was dressed in scrubs as he was allowed into theatre with me. Jane was also allowed with me and had changed into scrubs. I couldn't focus on anything. I was scared I was going to lose one or both of my babies.

Chapter 22

Cameron's POV

I was wheeled into theatre and transferred from the bed onto the operating table. I was hooked up to the monitors while the doctor was talking me through what would happen. It was checked to see if I could feel anything before my heart rate dropped sending doctors and nurses running to try and stabilise me. I was injected with more medication and finally Jane and Keiran were allowed in.

Dr Laine was performing the surgery and announced "5.59pm first incision made". Things moved quickly and I smelt burning flesh which had me gagging and Jane holding a kidney dish next to my face for me to vomit in if I needed. The anaesthesiologist adjusted the meds and I soon didn't feel like vomiting anymore. "Cameron, you might feel a pulling and tugging sensation, that's me trying to get the babies out and completely normal. You won't be in pain, it will just feel odd" Dr Laine said. "Ok" I replied. Keiran had a hold of my hand and was telling me how well I was doing throughout the procedure.

I felt the pulling and tugging and next minute we heard a cry. The sheet in front of my face was slightly lowered and I could see a baby.

"It's a boy" Keiran said. "No it's not, it's a girl" Jane said before taking the baby from Dr Laine and heading towards the side where there was a baby trolley waiting. She cleared the babies airways and got to measuring the babies weight and height calling it out to me as she went and recording it all on paper. I was watching her work and forgot there was another baby that needed to come out.

"More pulling and tugging now Cameron we have to get the second baby out" Dr Laine said. It snapped Keiran out of his trance and he was watching the sheet now like I was. We still had a hold of each other's hand. We heard another cry and I let a tear fall from my eyes. My babies were here now. I was a mum. The sheet was lowered again and I saw my little boy. There he was looking around and screaming. He wasn't happy at all. Another midwife came over taking him from Dr Laine over to Jane to clean him up and do the checks. "Congratulations Cameron. A baby girl born 6.13pm and a baby boy born 6.18pm on the 21st of January. Happy birthday babies" Dr Laine said.

"I did it. I did it" I said to myself. I had brought my babies into the world. I had tears in my eyes watching my babies. Keiran kissed my head and wiped my tears. "You did it Cam, I'm so proud of you" he said. The midwife picked up my baby girl and brought her over to us. "Here dad hold your little girl" she said handing my baby girl to Keiran who has a smile from ear to ear. I didn't bother correcting her at all, this moment was perfect and I didn't want to take that away from Keiran.

The midwife snapped a photo with Keiran's phone before going back over to Jane. Jane went to say something but I just shook my head. Jane walked over with my baby boy and laid him on my chest. My little boy snuggled into me and I wrapped my arms around him. He was perfect and so was my daughter. Jane laid my little girl on my chest too and Keiran sat back on the stool placing his hands on both of the twins backs. The midwife snapped a few photos of us all and congratulated us on our new additions.

Soon enough Jane took the twins informing me they needed to be checked in NICU as they were not breathing correctly. I burst into tears begging Keiran to stay with them and let my family know what was happening. He promised he would and left with Jane and the twins. I was stitched up and taken to recovery. I felt utterly alone at the moment and just hoped my babies were ok.

At about 9.30pm I was taken to a room where my family was waiting for me along with Max. They had flowers and teddies and congratulated me on the birth of the twins. I just burst into tears because I wanted to know if my babies were ok and no one had told me. "Why are you crying silly girl?" Lucy asked. She had stopped by taking over for Jane as she had been with me for 17 hours. "I don't know if they are ok, no one has told me. I just want my babies to be ok" I rushed out. Lucy laughed, "Cameron they are perfect. They are doing so well and I will bring them up as soon as you are settled. Keiran is with them and they both did a huge vomit bringing up the fluid they swallowed. All you need to worry about now is coming up with names for your twins" Lucy said. I just nodded my head and allowed her to check me out hooking me up to fluid and making sure I was settled.

Twenty minutes later Lucy and Keiran came into the room pushing the bassinets with the twins wrapped up sleeping soundly. I was in love. They looked like perfect little angels. I couldn't help but cry happy tears. Lucy said everyone had to leave shortly as it was way past visiting hours. They each took turns holding the twins and taking photos before congratulating me again.

"Keiran can stay the night" Lucy said before she left the room. "Do you mind me staying Cameron?" Keiran asked. I shook my head no. "Max you can come home with us. We will set you up in the spare room and can all come back tomorrow" dad said. They all kissed me and the twins goodbye before leaving. Keiran sat next to the bed and took my hand. "Thank you for letting me be part of this Cam. I'm so proud of you. You did it and they are perfect. What are you going to name them?" He asked. "How about Bodhi Keith after his dad for the boy and Darcy Rose after my mum for the girl?" I asked. "It's perfect Cam. Welcome to the family Bodhi and Darcy" Keiran said.

Epilogue

Cameron's POV

21st January, one year later.

I can't believe my babies are a year old now. The year has gone quickly and the twins are saying a few words including duck, mumma, Pa and key (Keiran). They are also walking well waddling around now. They get into everything now and it's hard to have them at work with me.

I expanded my business with some of the money I got from Keith's estate and now employ 3 full time staff while I work part time with the business side of things and do the paper work. The business was making money and I was making a profit. We now didn't need to do the markets anymore as we had a shop front and a huge online presence. We had expanded the kids range and included a womens range as well and we were busy which I was so thankful for.

The twins are having a birthday party today at my new house. I brought the place next door to my parents and we removed the fence between the properties creating a large backyard. We had jumping castles set up today and tables full of food and drinks under gazebos to block out the sun. We had number 1 balloons in pink and blue and Bodhi and Darcy each had there own cake.

I had made a few friends at the mothers group I attended with the twins, who were coming to help celebrate the twins turning one along with my family, Phil was bringing his new partner along as well, Max and Keiran were coming along with my workers and a couple of guys from the garage that I had got close to. Currently the twins were having a nap so they wouldn't be cranky for the party.

"Hey babe do you need a hand" Keiran asked before coming into the kitchen where I was cutting up fruit. "No I'm good" I replied. I forgot to mention that Keiran and I are a couple. He moved in with me after I brought this house to help with he twins and things just progressed from there. He still works and has an office at my warehouse which he works from. As he said he can literally work from anywhere as long as he has his computer and an internet connection.

At first we were worried what people would think of our relationship but our families were happy for the both of us. Well Maz wasn't and voiced her opinion in the media again. She had never met the twins and probably never would. She was a toxic person and we had no room for her in our lives. Max had brought a place closer to us as well as he wanted to be heavily involved in his grandchildren's lives and he was. Darcy and Bodhi adored "pa" and he adored them. We spoke to the twins about there dad and how much he loved them. I wanted the twins to know all about where they came from and how much they were loved. I even had photos of Keith in the twins bedroom.

Just as Keiran wrapped his arm around me the twins woke up. I laughed because Keiran always said they liked to cock block him. "I'll go" he said before kissing me. He was in for a surprise when he got them up. They were wearing special onesies with a message for Keiran on them that I had made.

"Babe" Keiran called out running back into the kitchen. My mum and dad had joined us by now and wondering why neither of us were getting the twins who were letting us know they wanted out of the cots. "Babe are you serious?" Keiran asked. I just nodded me head. "Seriously?" He asked again. Phil, his girlfriend and Max came into the kitchen to let us know people had started to arrive. "No way seriously?" Keiran asked again. "What's going on?" Max asked while my mum and dad headed into the twins room. "She is pregnant, Cameron is pregnant with another baby" Keiran rushed out coming towards me and pulling me into a bone crushing hug. "I love you Cameron" he said. "I love you too Keiran" I replied.

"We are expanding our family. Oh my god it's going to be crazy here in 9 months" Keiran laughed out. I shushed him. I didn't mind our family knowing but I didn't want the entire world to know just yet. "I want to shout it from the roof top. My family is growing. You have made me one happy son of a bitch" Keiran laughed out.

Our family congratulated us and we got the twins organised for the party. Keiran wouldn't let me lift anything and followed me around 'helping' so I didn't strain myself. I couldn't help but laugh at his behaviour. This was going to be a long pregnancy if he was reacting like this now. When the party was over and the twins settled Keiran pulled me aside. He caressed my stomach telling me how he couldn't wait to see it grow with our baby. He had treated the twins like his own children and I had no doubt in my mind that he would be just as great with our child.

"Babe, I can't thank you enough for everything. I love you and the twins more than I love myself. I know it's only been 9 months but I can't see myself anywhere but by your side. Marry me Cameron" he stated I nodded my head yes and our family cheered. I loved this man and we were happy in our little bit of paradise and the chaos we were creating. I couldn't wait to see what our future held but I knew we would be fine because we had family that supported us. I also know Keith would be happy because I had done what he asked and found love for the twins and I. I did forgive him for what he did and I hoped he knew that where ever he was now and I wished him nothing but eternal peace.

CPSIA information can be obtained
at www.ICGtesting.com
Printed in the USA
LVHW081531141222
735204LV00013B/636